SCRIPTURE

96

Rediscovering Vatican II

Series Editor: Christopher M. Bellitto, Ph.D.

Rediscovering Vatican II is an eight-book series in commemoration of the fortieth anniversary of Vatican II. These books place the council in dialogue with today's church and are not just historical expositions. They answer the question: What do today's Catholics need to know?

This series will appeal to readers who have heard much about Vatican II, but who have never sat down to understand certain aspects of the council. Its main objectives are to educate people as to the origins and developments of Vatican II's key documents as well as to introduce them to the documents' major points; to review how the church (at large and in its many parts) since the council's conclusion has accepted and/or rejected and/or revised the documents' points in practical terms; and to take stock of the council's reforms and paradigm shifts, as well as of the directions that the church appears to be heading.

The completed series will comprise these titles:

Ecumenism and Interreligious Dialogue: Unitatis Redintegratio, Nostra Aetate by Cardinal Edward Cassidy

The Church and the World: Gaudium et Spes, Inter Mirifica by Norman Tanner, SJ

The Laity and Christian Education: Apostolicam Actuositatem, Gravissimum Educationis by Dolores Leckey

Liturgy: Sacrosanctum Concilium by Rita Ferrone

Scripture: Dei Verbum by Ronald Witherup, SS

The Church in the Making: Lumen Gentium, Christus Dominus, Orientalium Ecclesiarum by Richard Gaillardetz

Evangelization and Religious Freedom: Ad Gentes, Dignitatis Humanae by Jeffrey Gros and Stephen Bevans

Religious Life and Priesthood: Perfectae Caritatis, Optatam Totius, Presbyterorum Ordinis by Maryanne Confoy, RSC

SCRIPTURE

Dei Verbum

Ronald D. Witherup, SS

Paulist Press
New York/Mahwah, NJ

Cover design by Amy King

Book design by Celine M. Allen

Library of Congress Cataloging-in-Publication Data

Witherup, Ronald D., 1950–
    Scripture : Dei Verbum / Ronald D. Witherup.
       p. cm. — (Rediscovering Vatican II)
    Includes bibliographical references and index.
    ISBN 0-8091-4428-X (alk. paper)
    1. Vatican Council (2nd : 1962–1965). Constitutio dogmatica de divina revelatione. 2. Revelation. 3. Bible—Study—Catholic Church. 4. Catholic Church—Doctrines—History—20th century. I. Title. II. Series.
    BX8301962.A45 D454 2006
    231.7'4—dc22
                                              2006008258

Published by Paulist Press
997 Macarthur Boulevard
Mahwah, New Jersey 07430

www.paulistpress.com

Printed and bound in the
United States of America

For Joseph A. Fitzmyer, SJ
Biblical exegete *par excellence*

CONTENTS

ACKNOWLEDGMENTS

I was a rather new and impressionable seminarian less than three years after the close of the Second Vatican Council. Although it took me some years to recognize the full significance of *Dei Verbum*, I can honestly say that the excitement of the renewal of a Catholic appreciation of the Bible encouraged by this inspiring constitution has never left me. Thus, when Paulist Press invited me to contribute this small volume to the Rediscovering Vatican II series, I was both honored to be asked and delighted to accept.

The series editor, Christopher Bellitto, deserves much credit for getting me to complete this book in a reasonable time frame. I thank him for his encouragement, patience, and gentle prodding. I also thank the staffs of the libraries of St. Mary's Seminary and University in Baltimore, Maryland, and St. Patrick's Seminary and University in Menlo Park, California, for assistance in obtaining numerous resources. In addition, my wonderfully supportive staff at the Provincial House deserves my gratitude, especially Thomas R. Ulshafer, SS, Gerald D. McBrearity, SS, and Judith Mohan. Their patience with my occasional disappearing act to work on the manuscript greatly enhanced my ability to focus on the project, and I thank them sincerely. I am also grateful to Michael Leach of Orbis Books for sending me an advance copy of the fifth volume of the Alberigo-Komonchak history of Vatican II. Although I could not incorporate references fully into the endnotes, its publication now rounds out the bibliographical entry of this magisterial history of the council. I also thank Professors Frederick J. Cwiekowski, SS, and John R. Donahue, SJ, for sharing helpful references, and Paul Zilonka, CP, for his dedicated service as *censor deputatus*. Any shortcomings that remain in the book are, of course, of my own making.

I also take the occasion to dedicate this work to Joseph A. Fitzmyer, SJ. He has been an inspiration to generations of biblical scholars. An indefatigable defender of the historical-critical method, an insightful commentator on the Bible and on magisterial teachings about the Bible, and a renowned expert in Aramaic, Father Fitzmyer embodies that rare blend of scholar's scholar and popular interpreter of the Bible. He incarnates the spirit of *Dei Verbum* and has been a faithful servant to the church in the exercise of his expertise. All who are truly interested in biblical studies owe him a great debt of gratitude for his tireless efforts to promote the Word of God.

Readers should note that the translation of *Dei Verbum* used herein, unless otherwise indicated, is from the Vatican website (www.vatican.va). I also consulted three other important translations (those of Norman Tanner, Austin Flannery, and Walter M. Abbott) listed in Further Reading. The Tanner translation is particularly useful because it contains both the Latin or Greek original and an English translation on facing pages. Finally, unless otherwise specified, the Bible translation is the New Revised Standard Version.

R. D. W.
Baltimore, Maryland
November 18, 2005

ABBREVIATIONS

Documents of Vatican II

AA	*Apostolicam Actuositatem* (Apostolate of the Laity)
AG	*Ad Gentes* (Missionary Activity)
CD	*Christus Dominus* (Bishops)
DH	*Dignitatis Humanae* (Religious Freedom)
DV	*Dei Verbum* (Revelation)
GE	*Gravissimum Educationis* (Christian Education)
GS	*Gaudium et Spes* (The Church in the World of Today)
IM	*Inter Mirifica* (Means of Social Communication/Mass Media)
LG	*Lumen Gentium* (The Church)
NA	*Nostra Aetate* (Non-Christian Religions)
OE	*Orientalium Ecclesiarum* (Eastern Catholic Churches)
OT	*Optatam Totius* (Priestly Formation)
PC	*Perfectae Caritatis* (Religious Life)
PO	*Presbyterorum Ordinis* (Ministry and Life of Priests)
SC	*Sacrosanctum Concilium* (Liturgy)
UR	*Unitatis Redintegratio* (Ecumenism)

Other Abbreviations

ABRL	Anchor Bible Reference Library
Alberigo, *Vatican II*	Giuseppe Alberigo and Joseph A. Komonchak, eds., *History of Vatican II*, 5 vols. (Maryknoll, NY: Orbis/ Leuven: Peeters, 1995–2005). See Further Reading for specific reference to sections on *Dei Verbum*.
Bea, *Word*	Augustin Bea, *The Word of God and Mankind* (Chicago: Franciscan Herald Press, 1967)
BETL	Biblitheca Ephemeridum Theologicarum Lovaniensium
BTB	*Biblical Theology Bulletin*
BibToday	*The Bible Today*

CBF	Catholic Biblical Federation
CCC	*Catechism of the Catholic Church*, 2nd ed. (Vatican: Libreria Editrice Vaticana, 1997)
ChicSt	*Chicago Studies*
DAS	*Divino Afflante Spiritu*
HomPastRev	*Homiletic & Pastoral Review*
IBC	*The Interpretation of the Bible in the Church*
ICEL	International Commission on English in the Liturgy
ITQ	*Irish Theological Quarterly*
JBL	*Journal of Biblical Literature*
NJBC	*The New Jerome Biblical Commentary*, ed. Raymond E. Brown, Joseph A. Fitzmyer, and Roland E. Murphy (Englewood Cliffs, NJ: Prentice-Hall, 1990)
PBC	Pontifical Biblical Commission
PD	*Providentissimus Deus*
PDV	*Pastores Dabo Vobis*
SubBi	*Subsidia Biblica*
TD	*Theology Digest*
TS	*Theological Studies*
USQR	*Union Seminary Quarterly Review*
Vorgrimler, *Commentary*	Herbert Vorgrimler, gen. ed., *Commentary on the Documents of Vatican II*, 5 vols. (New York: Herder and Herder, 1967–1969)

PREFACE

In the Middle Ages the primary way for Catholics to be exposed to the Bible was not through texts but through stone and stained glass. Since most people at the time were illiterate, they could not have read scriptural passages even if translations of the sacred writings had been available. In fact, until the age of Johann Gutenberg (ca. 1394–1468) and his justifiably famous printing press, books were not easily produced. Mass marketing was out of the question. Other than through occasional sermons and passion plays, the writings of the Bible remained outside the direct experience of most Christians. Instead, the great medieval cathedrals filled the gap. Their fabulous stone carvings and radiant stained glass windows allowed commoners to come into direct contact with stories of the Bible that illustrated Christian teaching.

One of the fondest memories of my first trip to the famous medieval cathedral at Chartres in France is spending a long time gazing at the incredible stained glass windows for which it is world-renowned. On the south transept wall, high above the level of the floor just below the rose window, is a set of lancet windows containing nine human figures. The central figure is Mary holding the child Jesus. Eight elegant figures flank her on both sides, four of whom sit on the shoulders of the other four. One has to study them carefully with the naked eye to read the names of these figures. Luckily, I had my small binoculars with me.

The four figures on the bottom, holding up their colleagues, are four prophets from the Old Testament: Jeremiah, Isaiah, Ezekiel, and Daniel. Perched on their shoulders, and thus able to gaze farther into the distance, sit the four evangelists: Luke, Matthew, John, and Mark, respectively. We might well imagine what an effective catechetical tool for the common faithful these colorful windows represented. Their message is as profound as their artistry is impressive. The Old Testament prophets are the foundation for the New Testament evangelists.

One cannot understand the New Testament without reference to the Old, while the Old Testament finds its true and deepest fulfillment in the New. The prophets foretold Christ; the evangelists recorded how Christ fulfilled their prophecies. Mary, as the primary means through which these prophecies were fulfilled, is the centerpiece of the tableau. No written explanation of this mysterious relationship between Old and New Testaments could be more efficacious.

This illustration helps to describe the integral relationship of the two Testaments of our Christian Bible. But I invoke the image here for another reason. It provides a colorful way to begin a reflection on the church's official teaching on the Sacred Scriptures, now more than forty years removed from the most dramatic doctrinal event of modern times, the Second Vatican Council (1962–1965).

The council's teaching was not shaped in a vacuum. Much theological reflection and formal teaching preceded it. In a sense, Vatican II's teaching on Scripture—embodied in *Dei Verbum*, the Dogmatic Constitution on Divine Revelation—rests on the shoulders of all that came before. Prior teachings provided a firm foundation and an orientation to doctrinal continuity. But the final product of Vatican II did not merely look to the past. It looked forward. Its firm foundations allowed the fathers of the council (i.e., the world's bishops) to look well into the future and thus orient the church in directions that were both traditional and innovative.

We speak here not only of the nearly two thousand years of Christian history, but also of the testimony of divine revelation in the entire Judeo-Christian tradition, which reaches back to our ancestor in faith, Abraham. Just as, in the medieval conception, the evangelists built upon their ancestors the prophets, so the fathers of the Second Vatican Council built upon their antecedents. They arrived at the first session of the council in Rome formed by their own training and pastoral experience as bishops. More important, hundreds of years of theology and church practice had shaped the church's life so strongly that many bishops must have envisioned any potentially dramatic changes at the council as almost unthinkable.

At the outset of this brief study, I should declare to readers my unbridled admiration for *Dei Verbum*. Luckily for me, I was a seminarian in the late 1960s and early 1970s at a time when the seminary faculty was emphasizing the need for absolute familiarity with the documents of Vatican II. The Dogmatic Constitution on Divine Revelation featured in several of my classes. Furthermore, I gleaned from my courses in Scripture that the professors had thoroughly absorbed the document's spirit as well as its clear instruction. They communicated to us students an excitement about the power of the Word of God that is hard to describe to those who did not experience the immediate aftermath of the council. My study of Scripture in those remarkable years was a true awakening. This happened, in large measure, because of the influence of *Dei Verbum* on Catholic biblical scholars, who happily published technical and popular works that disseminated for an eager Catholic public the results of modern biblical scholarship.

At this point, I should also note that differences of opinion exist over how best to interpret *Dei Verbum*, including how best to translate the Latin text. Archbishop William J. Levada, the prefect of the Congregation for the Doctrine of the Faith appointed in 2005 by Pope Benedict XVI, has stated that no *official* translation of *Dei Verbum* actually exists, although there are multiple and serviceable, if not definitive, translations in English. He expressed the hope that perhaps for the fiftieth anniversary in 2015 such an official translation might be forthcoming.

One can understand the desire for an official translation, since some problems of translation of *Dei Verbum* do exist. Yet the real issue is not merely one of translation. As with the Bible itself, frequent controversies erupt over *interpretation* of the text. Most scholars rightly suggest that just as important as translation is interpreting the conciliar text in its historical context. Essentially, this means applying modern scientific methods to the conciliar text itself to safeguard its historical origins. And there will always be a need to go back to the Latin original in order to ascertain its true meaning.

As we shall see, *Dei Verbum* has strengths and weaknesses. It is not a perfect document. Unlike some who claim that their faith has not been nourished by modern biblical studies that were largely encouraged by *Dei Verbum*, I must say that such biblical study has imbued my faith with a solid biblical foundation that has served me well for more than thirty years. And I have always sought to impart this positive outlook to the students and audiences I have addressed. I hope that this book, which commemorates the constitution's recent fortieth anniversary and looks forward to its fiftieth in 2015, may spark again some of the excitement that surrounded the constitution's appearance. Indeed, with the help of the Holy Spirit, enthusiasm for the Bible may blaze again and again for succeeding generations.

PART I
THE DOCUMENT

Setting the stage for Dei Verbum

Few of the participants at Vatican II imagined what a remarkable and transforming experience they were about to undergo when they arrived for the opening address by Pope John XXIII on October 11, 1962. Yet if they had any preconceptions that this council would be like its predecessor nearly a century earlier (Vatican I, 1869–1870), they would soon learn otherwise.

First of all, after the opening Mass to convene the council, a fifteenth-century Book of the Gospels was enthroned, as it would be for every general meeting of the council thereafter.[1] It provided a strong symbol of the authority of God's Word in directing the work of the council and the desire to be of service to the Gospel of Jesus Christ. Then, in his opening talk, titled *Gaudet Mater Ecclesia* ("Mother Church Rejoices"), the pope dismissed any notion that this would be a dogmatic type of council, intended to set out clearly once more time-honored truths that needed repetition in a modern, confused, and fast-paced world. He also distanced himself from naysayers and "prophets of doom, who are always forecasting worse disasters, as though the end of the world were at hand."

Instead, John XXIII raised the bar, so to speak, on expectations. His call for *aggiornamento* (an Italian word for "reform" or "updating") in the church dramatically changed the ecclesial world. He did not intend Vatican II to be another council to promulgate doctrines or restate traditional church teachings in more detail. Rather, the pope said,

What is needed at the present time is a new enthusiasm, a new joy and serenity of mind in the unreserved acceptance by all of the entire Christian faith, without forfeiting that accuracy and

1

precision in its presentation which characterized the proceedings of the Council of Trent and the First Vatican Council.
What is needed, and what everyone imbued with a truly
Christian, Catholic and apostolic spirit craves today, is that
this doctrine shall be more widely known, more deeply understood, and more penetrating in its effects on men's moral
lives. What is needed is that this certain and immutable doctrine, to which the faithful owe obedience, be studied afresh
and reformulated in contemporary terms. For this deposit of
faith, or truths which are contained in our time-honored
teaching, is one thing; the manner in which these truths are set
forth (with their meaning preserved intact) is something else.[2]

The pope was saying, in effect, that Vatican II was to be a *pastoral
council*.[3] Whereas previous councils had primarily defined dogmas
and doctrines or solidified moral practice, he envisioned that Vatican
II would reformulate church teaching in such a way that it would
appeal more broadly and more effectively to modern individuals. Even
divine revelation itself was not to be seen as a static, delimited deposit
of teachings but as a living body of truth. This was indeed something
new. It gave the council its direction for the next four years, and it led
to many behind-the-scene battles and discussions, both within and
without the *aula* (i.e., the hall, the nave of St. Peter's Basilica) where
the council fathers held their discussions and presentations.
No document characterizes this spirit of John XXIII more than
Dei Verbum. Some would judge it to be *the* characteristic document of
Vatican II. Pope Paul VI promulgated it on November 18, 1965, only
weeks before the end of the council on December 8, 1965, after a long
and tortuous period of formulation that encompassed all four sessions
of the council. Some may question which document of Vatican II has
had the most impact on Catholic life, but no one could say that *Dei
Verbum* has languished in obscurity. The topic of divine revelation is of
such importance that it is embedded at the center of many debates,
old and new. The fact is that *Dei Verbum* has had a major impact on
theology and biblical studies since its promulgation. Now that some
four decades have passed since its appearance, we are in a better position to assess its influence and to evaluate its efficacy.

By any estimation, *Dei Verbum* must be seen as a compromise document. It did not come into existence easily. As noted above, its history spanned the entire four years of the council. Indeed, we might say the council fathers underwent a difficult "labor" to give birth to this remarkable document. There were clearly divided camps among the council fathers and their theological experts or advisers (called *periti*; singular, *peritus*). One council father, Melkite Archbishop Neophytos Edelby of Edessa (Greece), opined in his diary that the "conservatives" were mostly from Italy and North America, while the "moderates" were from the rest of Europe and mission dioceses.[4] The terminology of conservative, liberal, or moderate can sometimes be misleading, and often people object to being placed in one category or another. Still, these categories remain the most useful in describing the poles of the conciliar discussions. The fact remains that even as the council began, factions existed that made it essentially a theological battleground. *Dei Verbum* inevitably reflects some of this tension.

The Dogmatic Constitution on Divine Revelation[5] did not appear out of nowhere. Its antecedents are long and somewhat complex. So, before looking at how the document itself came to be formulated during the council, we will sketch some broad influences that laid the groundwork for it. First we will look at a brief telescopic history of Catholic biblical interpretation. Then we will discuss the more immediate influences at work on the eve of the discussion of the first draft of the document. Finally, we will review the process that the document underwent to see the light of day.

A BRIEF HISTORY OF CATHOLIC BIBLICAL INTERPRETATION

From one perspective, we could say truthfully that the Catholic Church has always used the Bible as the Word of God in its teaching and moral practice. Already in the New Testament, one finds evidence that the early church venerated the Scriptures as God's Word and used them for teaching, preaching, and moral guidance (e.g., 2 Tim 3:15–16). For the first fifteen hundred years of its existence, the Catholic Church approached the Scriptures in a fairly uniform fashion.[6] People accepted them at face value. They were God's inspired

Word, God's primary revelation to the human family. They constituted the sacred canon (Greek, *kanōn*, "rule" or "reed"), the normative
texts for the life of the church. They were thus to be believed,
accepted, and taught as containing the truth, even in literal fashion.
The early church fathers wrote commentaries on many books of the
Bible, although they primarily concentrated on the spiritual meaning
of the text. Its basic historical accuracy was simply assumed. The Bible
served as a primary source book for prayer and piety. Yet, as time wore
on, the Bible actually came to function minimally in the church's daily
practice, despite the incorporation of a limited number of biblical
readings (in Latin) used at the Mass in the pre-Vatican II form of the
lectionary. Church teaching and pious spiritual practices overshadowed the Bible as a source of God's revelation, especially in the area of
morality.

The above picture was not entirely uniform, however. In the
twelfth and thirteenth centuries, for example, the Franciscans and
Dominicans were in the vanguard of reform movements within the
church that emphasized preaching as a means of spiritual renewal.
Bible stories featured prominently in their ministry. At a time when
sacramental and devotional aspects of Catholic piety had superseded
other practices, these groups designed preaching manuals, with illus-
trative stories from the Bible, to assist in their dynamic evangelical
ministry. Their approach was, of course, influenced considerably by
patristic interpretation of the Bible, especially that of St. Augustine,
yet they developed their own unique approach precisely at a time
when preaching to the faithful in Latin was losing its appeal.

Two names stand out in the fourteenth and fifteenth century, John
Wycliffe (1330–1384) and Jan Hus (1372–1415). Wycliffe is famous
for the English translation of the Latin Vulgate version of Bible that is
attributed to him (ca. 1382–1384), even though he did not accomplish
the task alone. His work signaled a strong interest in widening the
availability of the Bible through vernacular translations that could
appeal to the masses. In this regard, he influenced Hus, the Czech
reformer who opposed papal indulgences in his day and promoted the
Bible, along with church Tradition, as important for spiritual well-
being. He also emphasized preaching from the Bible and was interested in promoting vernacular translations. In the case of both figures,

however, the church viewed with fear their attempts to promote the Bible, and church authorities moved against them, considering them heretical. Hus was burned at the stake, along with his writings. Both men were essentially early precursors of the Protestant Reformation, especially in their earnest desire to promote the Bible.

In the sixteenth century, of course, the situation grew even more serious. With the disruption and in the aftermath of Martin Luther (1483–1546) and the Protestant Reformation, the Catholic Church began to define itself strictly over and against the Protestant tradition. Protestants emphasized the Word of God and promoted the Bible as the sole source of truth and revelation, containing all the teaching necessary for salvation. Catholics, on the other hand, defined themselves in terms of the sacraments and church teaching. This did not mean that the Catholic Church denied the importance of the Word of God. Rather, the church emphasized that its own authoritative teaching was equally necessary because the Bible was not self-evident in its teaching and did not encompass every aspect of divine revelation. The church saw itself as *the* authorized and faithful guide for discerning God's revelation in the world.

I should also add that from the perspective of professional study of the Bible, the Catholic Church also had its precursors to modern, scientific biblical interpretation. Most important, Richard Simon (1638–1712), a French Oratorian, was the first to recognize that oral traditions stood behind the written text of the Bible, an insight that went largely ignored in his day. He had great appreciation for the literary and historical aspects of Scripture that later generations of scholars would mine for great insights. For the most part, he and a few others represented early attempts at what would become the dominant, scientific approach to the Bible in the nineteenth and twentieth centuries.

I wish to highlight three comments in this overly brief summary of centuries of history. First, one of the strong factors that influenced Luther, who was himself an Augustinian priest, to challenge the Catholic Church concerning its avoidance of the Bible in its common practice was the Bible itself. Luther was a biblical scholar who had become enamored of the power of the Word of God in his own life, especially through the letters of St. Paul. He was understandably appalled that in his day priests received no formal training in Scripture and thus delivered sermons frequently devoid of any serious or detailed scriptural reflection. He saw this as a tremendous lack in the church, one that he set out to correct in ways that, unfortunately for church unity, got out of hand.

The second comment concerns the actual practice of the Catholic Church in the decades prior to Vatican II. The church, in fact, used Scripture frequently in its official documents and the like, especially with an eye toward "proof texting." This term signifies the practice of using biblical passages to justify, bolster, or "prove" one's position on any given topic. Most Christians have used the Bible in this fashion, an approach that continues into the present, but it was a regular feature of post-Reformation Catholicism. Catholics also employed the Bible routinely through another means, namely, the ancient monastic practice of the liturgy of the hours. This method of prayer utilized the psalms and biblical readings at specific times throughout the day as a means of consecrating one's day to God. The practice, however, was restricted largely to clerics and monks who were obligated to recite these prayers routinely as part of their commitment to priesthood and religious life.

A third comment is to emphasize that the church rarely taught that Catholics should not read the Bible. In practice, however, priests and nuns warned Catholics about the dangers of misinterpreting the Bible if one read it without official guidance. Catholics were seldom encouraged to pick it up and read it on their own, let alone use it for personal prayer or meditation. Some people have suggested from time to time that the Catholic Church never officially discouraged private reading of the Bible. But, in fact, as one scholar has pointed out, there are instances in which church authorities explicitly prohibited private study of Sacred Scripture for fear that doing so could lead to misinterpretation.[8]

While one can easily caricature the situation prior to Vatican II, this summary remains basically accurate. One scholar characterized the Catholic Church's attitude toward the Bible after *Dei Verbum* with words that reflect the position outlined above:

After centuries in exile the word of God once more occupies its central place in the life of the Catholic Church. The fact is beyond denying. One might even speak of the *rediscovery* of the word of God by the Catholic faithful who for centuries did not experience or practice a direct contact with the word of God and did not even have occasion to appreciate the value of that word for the life of faith.[9]

The fact is that the Catholic Church had been largely inattentive to the Bible for centuries. While we must acknowledge that some Catholic scholars quietly went about doing biblical research in the seventeenth, eighteenth, and nineteenth centuries, when scientific biblical studies began to flourish among Protestants, for the most part the church ignored, purposefully avoided, or sternly warned against these developments.

From an official standpoint, the church dealt with the Bible and the topic of divine revelation primarily through its official teachings. The Council of Trent (1545–1563) and Vatican Council I (1869–1870), in particular, issued declarations on these matters. (We will compare and contrast these councils with Vatican II in more depth below.) Trent (in the fourth session in 1546) confirmed the official canon of sacred writings contained in the Bible (forty-six books in the Old Testament; twenty-seven in the New Testament—in contrast to the Protestant acceptance of only thirty-nine books in the Old Testament, as in the Hebrew Bible). Also, in light of the Reformers' doctrine of *sola scriptura* (Scripture alone),[10] Trent affirmed the Catholic teaching that authoritative traditions outside the Bible could also contain authentic teachings that were to be obeyed and held in reverence.

With regard to revelation, Trent seemed to suggest that God had utilized two means to reveal his will to humanity, Sacred Scripture and Tradition. This, at least, became the common interpretation of Trent down through the nineteenth century. Later scholarship, however, demonstrated that this interpretation of Trent was flawed.[11] Trent spoke of divine revelation only in the context of its teaching on faith, and in that regard, it focused its attention on a strong reaction to the Protestant emphasis on the Bible as the sole source of revelation. The council had not actually taught that there were two separate sources of revelation. This notion, however, remained in circulation and provided a backdrop during the preparation for Vatican II and, specifically, for the first draft of *Dei Verbum*.

Vatican Council I had its own unique set of circumstances. It convened at the time of the dissemination of many new, "modern" scientific and historical ideas that were emerging in the wake of the Enlightenment. The publication of the German Lutheran scholar David Friedrich Strauss's book on Jesus in the New Testament (*Life of Jesus*, 1835) set off intense debates over the historical reliability of the Gospels. His book, among others, sparked heated debates over the relationship between history and myth in the Bible. One of the primary purposes of Vatican I was to condemn widespread "errors" that were burgeoning because of such scientific and academic developments. The council basically affirmed the teachings of the Council of Trent, especially those concerning the validity of the Bible and church traditions outside of the Bible, although it did not advance this question. The council went on to affirm the inspiration of Sacred Scripture by the Holy Spirit, calling God their author who ensures that they are "without error." Neither Trent nor Vatican I developed a thoroughgoing theology of revelation, but together they managed to solidify what was for centuries a specific approach to the question.

A small spark of change in the Catholic Church's position on the Bible slowly began to appear in the late nineteenth century. By the time of Pope Leo XIII (1810–1903), advances in scientific biblical studies had begun to make inroads in Catholic circles. We most likely remember Leo for his landmark encyclical on social matters, *Rerum Novarum* ("On Capital and Labor," 1891), which began a long line of Catholic teachings on social justice. But, in reality, Leo also made a significant contribution to biblical studies.

In 1893 Leo wrote an encyclical letter to address these issues forthrightly and to express some concerns. Titled *Providentissimus Deus* ("The God of All Providence"), this encyclical became the first major Catholic teaching in the "modern" era to address the topic of how Catholics should approach Sacred Scripture. The pope published it on the feast of St. Jerome (September 30), whose famous dictum "Ignorance of the scriptures is ignorance of Christ" could serve as the motto for Vatican Council II's own teaching on Sacred Scripture (*DV*, 25). Leo's encyclical largely reinforced the traditional Catholic approach to the Scriptures by emphasizing their basic historicity and accuracy as inspired documents. Scientific studies had begun to call into question the historical or scientific accuracy of some parts of the Bible, something the pope saw as dangerous. He essentially reiterated the church's longstanding tradition of biblical inerrancy, affirming that inspired texts could not contain any errors because they emanate from God.

Notwithstanding the above comments, Leo's encyclical allowed a small glimmer of a changing horizon to shine forth. He called on Catholic exegetes to use available scientific tools in their attempts to discern the meaning of the sacred texts, and he urged the teaching of biblical studies in seminaries and universities. He had an intense interest in promoting the Bible among Catholics, but in a way that would be responsible. To that end, later in his pontificate (1902) he formally established the Pontifical Biblical Commission (PBC), which was to become the official body of experts for handling matters pertaining to the Bible.

The PBC, in fact, played a major role in the developing Catholic approach to the Bible. Early in its history, the commission took a dim view of the modern scientific methods that scholars were applying to biblical interpretation. Indeed, the commission involved itself in giving opinions about many different issues confronting scholars at the beginning of the twentieth century. For example, between 1905 and 1915 the PBC sought to clarify the official Catholic position on many of these biblical questions. It issued a series of statements that many saw as reactionary, despite the nuance that some of the statements contained. In addition, the caution apparent in the PBC's stance ultimately led to the silencing or serious reprimand of numerous biblical scholars throughout the early twentieth century (e.g., Marie-Joseph Lagrange, Jules Touzard, Fulcran Vigouroux, among others).[12] We will return to the significance of this aspect of the PBC's history in Part Four. Suffice it to say here that these statements slowed the progress that *Providentissimus Deus* had heralded at least in a cautious manner.

Fifty years after the appearance of Leo XIII's letter, on the anniversary of its promulgation, Pope Pius XII issued a groundbreaking encyclical that most scholars consider to be the Magna Carta of Catholic biblical studies.[13] It was titled *Divino Afflante Spiritu* (*DAS*; "Inspired by the Divine Spirit," 1943). While it took its inspiration largely from *Providentissimus Deus*, it went far beyond it in terms of giving Catholic scholars the "green light" to pursue scientific biblical studies in earnest. The encyclical attempts to maintain a balance between the divine and human elements in the Bible while calling upon Catholic biblical scholars to use all appropriate scientific and linguistic means to ascertain the meaning of the sacred writings in a responsible and professional manner.

These two encyclicals, issued fifty years apart under very different circumstances, inadvertently ignited a firestorm of controversy that had both positive and negative consequences. Positively, Catholic biblical scholars in the late nineteenth and into the twentieth centuries took these papal clarion calls to heart and began to participate more earnestly and publicly in scientific biblical research. They began to read newer critical commentaries being published, especially in Germany and France, and to invest themselves in scholarly dialogues over such questions as the authorship of the Pentateuch (the first five books of the Bible), the oral and written origins of the Gospels, and the relationship between history and theology in the Bible.

Negatively, there was a strong reaction on the part of some Catholics —scholars, bishops, and laity—who attacked the results of this scientific study. A major focus became the validity of the historical-critical method, the primary scientific method of biblical study. Actually, this method is a series of related methodologies that undertake to distinguish historical and theological assertions in the Bible in the interest of reconstructing "what really happened." Some of the methods focus on oral and literary forms (e.g., form criticism, literary criticism), while others are concerned with the editing process the Scriptures underwent as they came into being (e.g., redaction criticism). We will revisit this method in more detail in Part Four, because it remains at the center of current biblical discussions.

One clear indication that the controversy about how to interpret the Bible would lurch to and fro is found in Pope Pius XII's promulgation in 1950 of an encyclical on biblical inspiration titled *Humani Generis* ("On the Human Race"). Issuing this encyclical only seven years after *Divino Afflante Spiritu*, the pope expressed concerns that some interpreters were going too far, especially regarding the theory of evolution, which he said was unproven and only a theory. He strongly warned against the theory of polygenism (i.e.,) that Adam and Eve were not the sole original ancestors of the human race), but avoided an outright condemnation of it. Some might read this encyclical as an attempt (to halt) the scientific advances so encouraged by the same pope's earlier encyclical *Divino Afflante Spiritu*. While it is true that the tone of *Humani Generis* is (not) as (positive) as that of the earlier encyclical, the lack of any direct condemnation of biblical scholars is noteworthy. Moreover, the pope still encouraged scientific research and discussion regarding the theory of evolution. In other words, the encyclical did not seriously hamper scholarly research, nor did it redirect the course of biblical studies set into motion by *Divino Afflante Spiritu*. But it was a little bump in the road.

Some see in this ebb and flow within the Catholic Church's official stance toward biblical scholarship as characteristic of a repressive institution. But perhaps it is more due to the slow and difficult pace of change that happens after centuries of uniformity. In any case, these controversies not only persisted throughout the period of the Second Vatican Council, but they continue into the present, something we will address in Part Four.

IMMEDIATE INFLUENCES PRIOR TO *DEI VERBUM*

The developments outlined above set the stage for the consideration of a document like *Dei Verbum* at Vatican II. But there were things going on backstage shortly before the council convened that were to have enormous impact on the shape of the document. Two influences stand out: the biblical movement and the liturgical movement.

The Biblical Movement

The debates of the mid-nineteenth and early twentieth centuries over the historical reliability of the Scriptures form the immediate backdrop of *Dei Verbum*. The term "biblical movement" designates a rather broad reality encompassing the scientific awakening taking place among Catholic biblical scholars in the first half of the twentieth century. The rapid acceptance of the historical-critical method among Protestant scholars had begun to have a wider impact on Catholic scholars, and slowly upon the general public, in ways that frightened leaders in the Catholic Church.

As we mentioned above, a natural preoccupation of historical criticism was the attempt to establish bedrock history in the Bible. The spiritual message of the Sacred Scriptures took a back seat to other questions. What really happened at creation? Do the stories of Genesis 1–11 recount literal history? How did the Exodus event really take place? Did Moses himself write all first five books of the Bible? (That would be a pretty remarkable accomplishment, since he died before all the events recounted in the books had taken place!) What really lies behind the miracle stories of Jesus in the Gospels? How much theological influence, based on the faith of the early church, has shaped the New Testament writings? Questions of this sort began to take center stage. They also led to what became known as "the quest for the historical Jesus," which in turn became preoccupied with trying to ascertain which of the four Gospels was the earliest and, presumably, the closest in time to and the most accurate account of the life of the "historical Jesus." The problem was that the more scholars investigated the Gospels, the more the outcomes led to skepticism about the historical reliability of the texts.

In time, two large, amorphous camps of scholars formed along doctrinal lines, including in the Catholic Church. There were those who saw in the historical-critical method hope for making progress on our historical understanding of the Bible. They did not see this as a threat to faith but as a natural outcome of intellectual curiosity and a search for the truth. Others, however, including Popes Pius IX and Leo XIII, saw grave danger in these developments and sought to stave them off. They feared that such historical questioning would lead to a serious erosion of faith primarily because they call into question the inerrancy of the Bible. If God is the author of Sacred Scripture, how could it not be totally (including historically) accurate?

This division existed right down to the eve of Vatican II, and indeed continues in our own day. The history of Catholic biblical scholarship throughout the first half of the twentieth century is a bit like the dance of life, two steps forward, one step back. Scholars would publish the findings of their research on some of these biblical questions, only to be attacked as undermining the faith. Even as Vatican II got under way, such actions were still being taken against biblical scholars who had come under suspicion for questionable positions (e.g., Edward Siegman in the United States, and Maximilian Zerwick and Stanislas Lyonnet in Rome). Two cardinals loomed large in this division, and they would make a major impact on the shape of *Dei Verbum.* In favor of the newer approaches to biblical studies was Cardinal Augustin Bea, a German biblical scholar who presided over the Vatican's Secretariat for Promoting Christian Unity, charged with coordinating the Vatican's outreach to other Christians. His outspoken opponent was the influential Italian Cardinal Alfredo Ottaviani, prefect of the Holy Office (formerly "The Holy Office of the Inquisition"). These two monumental figures of the Roman curia (i.e., the administrative offices of the Vatican) symbolize the division about biblical interpretation that was in place as the council prepared to begin its work in October 1962.

In short, the biblical movement found itself split into opposing camps who saw in the prospect of an ecumenical council the possibility of fostering their particular approach to the Bible because of modern developments. The camps were represented not only by scholars themselves who were split on the issues, but also by the cardinals and bishops who were to assemble in Rome for the council. In particular, the shape of the questions formed by the biblical movement squarely focused on the relationship between Sacred Scripture and Tradition, broadly seen as the authoritative teachings of the church. As we shall see, this became the lightning rod for subsequent discussions at the council.

The Liturgical Movement

At the same time that biblical studies were fermenting among Catholic scholars, liturgical scholars were creating waves of their own. The "liturgical movement" is more appropriately discussed at length in the volume in this series on the Constitution on the Sacred Liturgy (*SC*). Yet as both that document and *Dei Verbum* make clear, there is an intimate and crucial connection between Word and sacrament in the Catholic tradition. *Sacrosanctum Concilium* was one of the first two documents approved by the fathers of the council (Dec. 4, 1963). Perhaps it is no accident that liturgy became an early focus of the council. Liturgy, especially Sunday Mass, is where the majority of Catholics encounter their faith in a regular and concrete fashion.

The liturgical movement, like the biblical movement, was very broad and centered primarily in universities, especially in Belgium and France. In the United States it was most identified with St. John's Abbey (Benedictine) in Collegeville, Minnesota, where Virgil Michel and his associates founded an important liturgical magazine, *Orate Fratres* (later called *Worship*). Michel was a monk at the abbey; he and his brilliant student Godfrey Diekmann became very influential in the field of liturgy, and Diekmann served as a *peritus* at Vatican II. The study of the history of liturgy had led these scholars to realize that the Roman rite had gained so many accretions over the centuries that it was no longer as meaningful to modern-day Catholics as it had once been. For one thing, Latin had long disappeared from common parlance. The Mass, while universally celebrated in the same fashion and Latin language throughout the world, needed dramatic renovation. Indeed, the Constitution on the Sacred Liturgy expressly announced that the church would "undertake a careful general reform of the liturgy" precisely so that people could more properly benefit from it spiritually (*SC*, 21).

A large part of this task would be, the council announced, the revision of the liturgical books, most especially those containing the biblical readings and prayers used at all liturgical functions. This would lead to the drawing up of liturgical texts in the vernacular, that is, in modern languages such as French, Italian, Spanish, German, English, and so on, rather than Latin. The document also drew specific attention to the centrality of Sacred Scripture in this process (*SC*, 24). Bishops and experts would be called upon to begin this urgent task (*SC*, 25) so that the faithful would be renewed in their spiritual lives. This would also require renewal of the role of Scripture in the life of the church (*SC*, 51), something that would be specifically addressed in *Dei Verbum*.

In a sense, the biblical and liturgical movements together gave a significant push to the issues that eventually coalesced in *Dei Verbum*.

THE PROCESS OF APPROVING *DEI VERBUM*

The story of how this remarkable document came into being makes for fascinating reading. Its history is replete with theological intrigue. Unfortunately, it is too long and complex for this book, so the condensed version will have to suffice. One can consult the larger histories of Vatican II for more details and information on the key figures of the discussions.[14] I summarize the short story of *Dei Verbum* artificially in four stages: a preparatory phase, followed by three successive stages of various drafts. To assist with keeping track of the various editions of the constitution, I provide a chart on page 29 that readers can consult as we summarize this story.

Stage One: The Preparatory Phase

To begin, one must remember that John XXIII charged the cardinals and their assistants in the Roman curia with much of the preparation for the council. This was understandable, since they were the administrators at the Vatican. (The main offices are now called "congregations" or "councils," or generically "dicasteries.") Already in 1959 the Holy Office, under the direction of Cardinal Ottaviani and with the assistance of that dicastery's secretary, Jesuit Father Sebastien Tromp, had begun consultations to prepare for the council. A preparatory Theological Commission, one of ten that would draft various proposals for the council, was formed. It was composed of numerous bishops assisted by expert theologians. They were charged with preparing a major document on revelation. Their intention clearly was to draft a statement that would reinforce strongly the teaching of Vatican I and Trent on revelation. Ottaviani expected that the constitution would quickly be approved by the council fathers during the first session of the council (October 11–December 2, 1962). But the process became much more involved than he or his supporters ever expected.

We should keep in mind that during this preparatory phase the Vatican initiated a massive consultation of the world's bishops to search for important topics to bring before the ecumenical council. Bishops were asked to submit their suggestions (Latin, *postulata*) in writing, and several bishops' conferences began to consult with theologians for help in understanding many current issues that had emerged in recent decades. Some of these theologians would be called on to attend the council as *periti*, and their ideas would profoundly affect many of the council's decrees, most especially *Dei Verbum*. It is clear, however, that many of the world's bishops thought the council would reinforce earlier church teachings. Few expected the kinds of dramatic discussions that would take place and lead to the changes that were to overtake the Catholic world after the council ended.

Stage Two

The second stage was the presentation of a draft of the document (technically called a "schema") during the first session of the council. The first schema was titled, "A Schema of a Dogmatic Constitution of the Sources of Revelation." It contained five chapters:

Chapter 1. The Double Source of Revelation

Chapter 2. The Inspiration, Inerrancy and Literary Form of Scripture

Chapter 3. The Old Testament

Chapter 4. The New Testament

Chapter 5. Holy Scripture in the Church

Since the Holy Office had been the chief architect of the document during the years 1960–1962, its tone reflected the concerns of Ottaviani and his supporters. The first schema was designed to reiterate in forceful terms the basic teaching on revelation as pronounced by the councils of Trent and Vatican I. The schema's outline demonstrates this, as is evident in the title of the first section. Relying on an outdated understanding of prior councils, especially the Council of Trent, it addresses the "two sources" of revelation. The framers of the document intended to bolster the notion that the church's Tradition constituted a comparable, authoritative source of divine revelation, and to reinforce the church's teaching on biblical inspiration and inerrancy. They viewed revelation primarily as a "deposit" of faith, a defined set of dogmas and doctrines that could be clearly delineated and upheld as revealing God's will (e.g., the literal sense of the expression "guard the deposit" in 1 Tim 6:20; 2 Tim 1:14). The two sources, of course, were understood to be the Word of God and the Tradition of the church.

Curiously, as we have noted above, the drafting of the first schema was actually more a product of a certain preconceived theology than it was an accurate reflection of the teaching of Trent and Vatican I. The entire approach emerged from a misreading of the teaching of Trent. As (then) Father Joseph Ratzinger, a *peritus* for the German bishops at the council, pointed out, the draft was essentially "a canonization of Roman school theology" and did not acknowledge the living Tradition of the church.[15] Nonetheless, this type of approach had become entrenched in some of the theological schools in Rome, where some professors viewed the advances of biblical studies as a serious threat to the faith.

Ottaviani presented this first schema to the bishops at the council in the fall of 1962 and offered his own favorable assessment of it. Immediately—much to his surprise and that of his supporters—several important bishops rose, one after another, to offer stinging criticisms of the schema. The elderly and distinguished archbishop of Lille (France), Cardinal Achille Liénart, delivered a scathing assessment of the schema, declaring tersely in Latin, the language of the council interventions, "*Hoc schema non mihi placet*" (I do not accept this schema). Cardinals Joseph Frings (Cologne), Paul Léger (Montreal), Franz König (Vienna), Bernard Alfrink (Utrecht), Leo Suenens (Brussels), Joseph Ritter (St. Louis), and Augustin Bea himself followed Liénart and expressed dissatisfaction with the schema. Bea was quite clear that he wanted a schema that would be more ecumenical in tone, shorter and more precise, and more supportive of modern biblical scholars.

The objections of these major figures were apparently prepared independently, yet their opinions coalesced into a strong signal that the schema designed by the Theological Commission, and shepherded by Ottaviani, was wrong-headed. The objections were not merely to the document's tone. They had just as much to do with its content.

Some critics expressed dissatisfaction with the schema because it did not reflect the results of newer scientific methods of biblical studies. Moreover, the Belgian bishop Paul Emile De Smedt (Bruges), who worked for Bea in the Secretariat for Christian Unity, bemoaned the fact that the schema did not have any of the ecumenical tone that the secretariat had advised the Theological Commission to incorporate. More important, there was concern over certain elements in the document's description of Scripture and Tradition. There was great dissatisfaction with the fact that they were conceived of as two separate sources. Also at issue was whether revelation should be said to have stopped with the death of the last apostle. Another concept caused concern as well, namely, the "material sufficiency of Scripture" (i.e., the view that Scripture itself can be said to contain the fullness of revelation). Some thought that the schema should not treat this topic at all, but that it should be left to further discussion by theological experts.

American interveners offered a somewhat mixed viewpoint.[16] Cardinal Joseph Ritter (St. Louis) explicitly called for a rejection of the schema, while Cardinal James McIntyre (Los Angeles) supported it. Cardinal Albert Meyer (Chicago) supported Bea's call for a new schema, adding that he wished a new draft would include more mention of the late Pope Pius XII who had been such a supporter of biblical scholarship. Meyer also gets the credit for being the first to raise the issue of the inadequacy of the section on inerrancy, a point that others supported.[17] An auxiliary bishop of New York, James Griffiths, offered a kind of compromise. He wanted to retain the positive elements of the schema but also asked for wider consultation among experts so that the final product could be improved and made more practical.

Ratzinger later summarized the dissatisfaction with the draft in this fashion:

> The text was, if one may use the label, utterly a product of the "anti-Modernist" mentality that had taken shape about the turn of the century. The text was written in a spirit of condemnation and negation. . . . The same cramped thinking, once so necessary as a line of defense, impregnated the text and informed it with a theology of negations and prohibitions; although in

themselves they might well have been valid, they certainly could not produce that positive note which was now to be expected of the Council.[18]

There were also, of course, defenders of the schema. Cardinals Fernando Quiroga y Palacios (Santiago de Compostela), Ernesto Ruffini (Palermo), and Giuseppe Siri (Genoa) strongly defended the draft. They tried ardently to persuade others to accept their position. Finally, after much discussion, the vote took place on November 20, 1962, but in an unusual form. Indeed, this incident was one of the most confusing in the council's history, and it still causes heads to spin.

Instead of using the normal voting categories of *placet* (yes), *non placet* (no), and *placet iuxta modum* (yes with reservation) regarding the controversial schema, the council fathers were asked to vote simply either to halt the discussions or to continue. The problem was that this change in the formulation of the vote confused many of the council fathers. Several bishops called for an explanation of the procedure. Even after further attempts to clarify the procedure, confusion still reigned among the bishops. One bishop from the United States, Robert Tracy (Baton Rouge), admitted in his diary that he himself had not voted the way he had intended, and he was sure many others—on both sides of the question—had done the same.[19] Nevertheless, an extremely large number of bishops voted to halt the discussion (1,368 yes; 822 no; 19 invalid votes), but the number was not large enough to satisfy the requisite two-thirds majority. In essence, the vote not to continue the debate indicated a resounding rejection of the schema. But the lack of the required two-thirds majority created a dilemma: what would happen now?

Although it looked as if the draft would have to suffice and discussions would have to continue, Pope John XXIII himself intervened the next day and, in a brilliant stroke of the diplomacy for which he was famous, remanded the draft to an entirely new working group. He named Cardinals Ottaviani and Bea as the two chairmen of this ad hoc committee (the "mixed commission") and appointed various bishops from the Holy Office and the Secretariat for Christian Unity as members. He also appointed Father Sebastien Tromp and Msgr. Johannes Willebrands (later a cardinal), respective secretaries of the two dicasteries, as secretaries of the mixed commission. In essence, the pope forced the two opposing camps to sit down and work things out. They subsequently hammered out an extensive revision of the schema, which was to lead to more discussions.

Perhaps more important than the actual defeat of the first schema of this constitution was the implicit political ramification of this action. No one knows for certain what factors led John XXIII to take such a momentous step of direct intervention in the process.[20] His decision, however, essentially signaled a curtailment of the influence of the officials of the Roman curia who had been attempting to engineer the council according to their own well-conceived plan. The unexpected rejection of this crucial draft document indicated that John XXIII had, in essence, allowed the fathers of the council to override the curia. This was indeed a signal that Vatican II would be no rubber-stamp council on the matter of revelation and Sacred Scripture nor, as it turned out, on a number of other topics and documents.

Stage Three

The third stage in the process spanned a lengthy period of time. It involved the design and presentation of two more drafts of the document, formulated by the special Doctrinal Commission of the council at the second and third sessions of the council (1963, 1964, respectively). Actually, during the second session there was no plenary discussion of the second draft. Rather, the process allowed for written recommendations (called in Latin *animadversiones*) to be submitted. For a brief time, some bishops promoted a movement at the council to have the topic of revelation treated in the Constitution on the Church rather than in a separate document. This would have, in fact, followed the practice of Trent and Vatican I. But Pope Paul VI (elected June 21, 1963), who had by then succeeded John XXIII, rejected this idea. As a cardinal, he had earlier expressed the notion that this constitution would be decisive for the council, so he had it placed again on the agenda.

The title for the second schema, "On Divine Revelation," reflected the dramatic change that had occurred since the rejection of the first schema. Gone was the notion of the "two sources" and, in its place, a new emphasis on the revealed Word of God appeared. The outline of the second schema was as follows:

Prologue   개시된 하느님의 말씀

Chapter 1. The Revealed Word of God

Chapter 2. The Divine Inspiration and Interpretation of Sacred Scripture

Chapter 3. The Old Testament

Chapter 4. The New Testament

Chapter 5. The Use of Scripture in the Church

Already one could perceive the shift in emphasis that the new schema embodied. However, because of the press of other council business, and because the schema was still in the process of being revised, the council fathers never debated it in the aula. Instead, focus shifted to the Decree on Religious Liberty (*DH*), which, amazingly enough, would help refocus *Dei Verbum* even further because of its own emphasis on ecumenical dimensions of religious freedom.[21]

In the meantime, bishops submitted multiple suggestions to improve the draft, which they already viewed as a great advance over its predecessor. The process led to a third schema, titled "Dogmatic Constitution on Divine Revelation," which the council fathers discussed at length at the third session of the council. It is interesting to see how the intervening discussions and written suggestions had changed the direction of the document by 1964. Although closely resembling the outline of the second schema, the new schema nonetheless reflected refinements that would shape the final document. Its outline was:

Prologue

Chapter 1. Revelation Itself

Chapter 2. The Transmission of Divine Revelation

Chapter 3. The Divine Inspiration and the Interpretation of Holy Scripture

Chapter 4. The Old Testament

Chapter 5. The New Testament

Chapter 6. Holy Scripture in the Church's Life

This schema emphasized a more personalized view of revelation and did not focus as much on revelation as a deposit of doctrines. It also placed Scripture and Tradition on equal footing as one source of God's self-revelation to humanity, but with aspects specific to each category. One can also see in the slight change of wording in the last chapter a turn toward a more pastoral approach to the question of revelation. The essential elements that would appear in the final schema were falling into place.

The discussion during the third session of the council (September and October, 1964) was in-depth but began on a tone that was quite different from that of the first time around in 1962.[22] Cardinal Léger of Montreal rose to affirm his basic satisfaction with the new schema, especially because it was more biblical in orientation. Others added positive comments. Cardinal Juan Landázuri Ricketts (Lima) spoke in favor of the new draft in the name of the Peruvian Episcopal Conference, and many bishops followed suit to express their basic support of the document. As the days of the debate wore on, there were nonetheless recommendations for changes.

The question of the material sufficiency of Scripture became a focus again. One intervention, given by Luciano Rubio, the prior general of the Augustinian Hermits, called for the question to be presented in two separate ways: (1) whether there are revealed truths apart from Scripture, and (2) whether Tradition declares revealed truths that have a basis in Scripture but perhaps have other foundations as well. Christopher Butler, the abbott president of the English Benedictines and a theological adviser at the council, who also gave several significant interventions, argued against trying to resolve the issue of the material sufficiency of Scripture in the text. He believed that the theological discussions within the church had not yet come to resolution on the matter. He thus preferred that the issue be left open. Later, in another intervention, Butler argued vigorously to keep the positive references to the modern historical-critical method in the constitution (*DV*, 19), when it seemed that some council fathers mistrusted this orientation.

Many other interventions provided input on one part of the schema or another, but primarily as ways to improve rather than reject the draft. Several outstanding presentations made an impact on the council. One was by the Cardinal Albert Meyer (Chicago), who had the advantage of an excellent *peritus* in the person of the legendary Passionist Father Barnabas Ahern, who was the only American biblical scholar *peritus* at the council. Meyer's multiple presentations at the council were remembered for their balanced approach and theological erudition.

Regarding the third schema of the constitution, Meyer particularly affirmed the shape of the second chapter. In particular, commenting on chapter 2 of the draft, he said that he appreciated the presentation of Tradition as "something alive, dynamic and whole, i.e., consisting not only of doctrinal declarations but also of the cult and practice of the entire Church."[23] At the same time, however, he pointed out that there are sometimes limitations to church Tradition, which can always be subject to deeper reflection, and the constitution did not acknowledge this sufficiently. He advised that the constitution incorporate some acknowledgment of this reality in the text. Regarding chapter 3, Meyer asked for further revision on the question of inspiration, because he felt that the draft did not progress much further than Leo XIII's encyclicals on the topic.[24] Meyer's views found general acceptance among many of the council fathers and helped to influence the final schema.

The question of inspiration and inerrancy to which Meyer drew attention also preoccupied Indian Bishop Francis Simons (Indore). He detected in the draft a kind of circular argument in which inspiration and inerrancy were being posed of one another.[25] He called attention to the existence of mistakes in Scripture that should not in any way be considered as detracting from the overall inspiration of the Bible. This would prove to be one of the sticking points of the constitution that would lead to compromise language on the question of the relationship between inspiration and inerrancy. It also became one of the critical issues in later struggles to interpret the constitution, as we shall see in Parts Three and Four.

Another significant intervention was made by the Melkite archbishop, Neophytos Edelby, who used his Eastern rite perspective to great effect.[26] Focusing on article 12 of the schema, he pointed out that too much of the polemics from the Counter-Reformation were still reflected in the draft in the discussion of inspiration. He emphasized the Bible as both a liturgical and prophetic work, not just a written record of revelation. Using insights from the Eastern rite, which gives extraordinary emphasis to the invocation of the Holy Spirit who enables the consecration of bread and wine into the Body and Blood of Christ, he compared the Scriptures to a similar kind of consecration, in which the human words become the sacred Word of God. It is the mysterious action of the Holy Spirit that guides this transformation.[27] He also emphasized the importance of interpreting the Bible within the context of all of salvation history. Many bishops received Edelby's intervention with great appreciation, although its ultimate effect on the final form of the constitution is debatable.[28]

Not all interventions concerned the doctrinal issues in the constitution. The German bishop Herman Volk (Mainz), for instance, emphasized the importance of chapter 6 of the constitution. From his perspective, the pastoral application of the constitution was very important for a proper understanding of it.[29] His words differed somewhat from those of the Spanish bishop Pablo Barrachina Estevan (Orhuela-Alicante) who had spoken the previous day and expressed dissatisfaction with the pastoral dimensions of the last chapter.[30] He called for a more transcendent aspect of the Word to dominate the pastoral practice of the faithful, and for the ecclesial dimension of Scripture not to be lost. Interventions such as these pointed to the desire of many bishops to produce documents that would genuinely impact the lives of the faithful and not simply repeat erudite doctrinal teachings that might have little to do with the lives of ordinary Catholics.

Sometimes vestiges of bygone arguments reappeared. For example, Italian bishop Constantino Caminada (Ferentino) warned against promoting the distribution of the Scriptures among the faithful because they might not interpret them correctly. A Yugoslavian bishop, Smiljan Cekada (Skolja) was concerned that the constitution spoke too optimistically about the ability of the laity to benefit from Scripture without the aid of more direct guidance from the magisterium (the official teaching authority of the church). He also expressed skepticism about the effectiveness of many modern translations and about the call in chapter 6 for ecumenical cooperation in order to produce good translations.[31]

Yet, overall, one can see that the council fathers received this schema much more positively than the first one. The tone of the bishops had entirely shifted. They no longer focused on merely the negative but were earnest in their desire to improve a document that they already perceived was headed in the right direction. The discussion at this point set the stage for final considerations during the last session of the council. One German Jesuit theologian, Josef Neuner, summarized the movement from the first to the third schema in this way: "...in the first draft, [the schema on revelation] became a symbol of disagreement; in the second, an attempt at reconciliation; in its third form, a positive exposition of the nature of revelation and its presence in the Church."[32] This is a very fair assessment of the incredible transformation the schema underwent.

Stage Four

The fourth and final stage in the process actually consisted of two steps that ultimately led to the final schema. The first step of the process evolved outside the formal setting of the council itself.

Because at Vatican II so many of the questions regarding revelation concerned the Bible, and in light of the newer scientific tools that had emerged in historical criticism, the PBC set out in the midst of the council to issue a document of its own on the historicity of the Gospels. This was, of course, a thorny matter that had caused much of the anxiety of those opposed to the use of historical criticism by Catholic exegetes. The PBC, in fact, was concerned that the battle for promoting modern biblical methods of inquiry might be lost if the point was not strengthened.

On April 21, 1964, the PBC issued its document, titled "Instruction on the Historical Truth of the Gospels." The instruction is sometimes referred to by its Latin title, *Sancta Mater Ecclesia* ("Holy

Mother Church"). The significance of this highly nuanced document should not be underestimated. It put into a broader context the conciliar discussions taking place over the historical foundations of the biblical data, and it explicitly recognized the existence of differing layers of tradition in the Gospels. Specifically, the document speaks of information in the Gospels originating in the "life situations" of three distinct time periods:

1. the time of Jesus
2. the time of the apostolic preaching
3. the time of the evangelists

This framework shows the influence of the historical-critical method of biblical interpretation. Scholars use form criticism to discern evidence from the first two time periods, in which they seek to identify the various "forms" preserved in the oral traditions about Jesus (miracle stories, teachings, narratives, hymns, doxologies, prayers, and so on). Likewise they use redaction criticism to work with the third stage of the development of the gospel traditions in identifying the particular interests, themes, and concerns of the evangelists and their respective communities as well as those of later audiences, such as Gentile Christians.

This approach was significant both in promoting the value of responsible historical criticism (though the PBC warned of exaggerated forms of the method) and in recognizing that the Gospels were not written at the time of Jesus himself but decades later. There was a long period of oral, written, and edited traditions that eventually created the final form of the Gospels as they exist in our canon. This formulation of the PBC made its way into the final form of *Dei Verbum* (articles 12 and 19), and leads us to the final phase of the formation of the document. In fact, many scholars mark the publication of this document as a turning point in the production of the constitution precisely because the instruction's enlightened approach would influence the final production of the constitution.

The second step of this last stage was the presentation of the third schema with revisions. This first edition of the final schema of *Dei*

Verbum underwent numerous discussions and votes by the council fathers that led to various revisions before the production of a final edition. In fact, when the first edition of the final schema was presented to the council fathers, it evoked nearly fifteen hundred votes of *placet iuxta modum*, indicating that there was still some dissatisfaction with wording.[33] Even this late in the process the bishops made many suggestions to improve the document.

Moreover, Pope Paul VI himself, as he had done for the Decree on Ecumenism (*UR*) in 1964, submitted a few suggestions for the final emendations of the constitution. On October 6, 1965, he sent to the council fathers a letter that Cardinal Ottaviani presented. In it the pope made seven suggestions for changes in the text, especially in chapters 2 and 3 of the constitution. Most of them were minor, except for one emendation in article 9 of chapter 2 where the pope asked for slight changes on the issue of the material sufficiency of Scripture in order to make the text more ecumenically desirable.[34] This addressed the same vexing question that the council fathers had struggled with in prior heated exchanges, and it shows just how difficult it was to bring it to a successful conclusion. However, at a vote on October 29, 1965, the revised schema received 2,081 *placet* and only 27 *non placet* votes, but with a few more revisions recommended. The extended process was nearing its end.

At last, on November 18, 1965, the council voted on the final form of the schema, which only near the end of the process received the title "*Dei Verbum*," which Joseph Ratzinger labeled "one of the happiest formulations in the text" because of its emphasis on the Word of God.[35] The vote was overwhelmingly positive in favor of the document (2,344 out of 2,350 votes), and Pope Paul VI immediately signed and promulgated it the same day. The final text clearly represented a victory for biblical scholarship within the church. The long, arduous process begun four years earlier had finally reached its conclusion. As one historian put it, "In *Dei Verbum*, the Church officially espoused historical criticism and placed itself squarely in the mainstream of biblical scholarship."[36] The constitution would breathe fresh life into the biblical movement in the Catholic Church for decades, but it would also lead to further controversies, not the least of which was over how to interpret the dogmatic constitution itself.

Summary

Although I have chosen to summarize the process recounted above in four stages, the successive drafts of *Dei Verbum* make a reconstruction far more complex. Alois Grillmeier, an expert on the council, has summarized the process by means of a convenient, if sometimes confusing, system of designations that are worth reiterating here.[37] He designated each successive schema of the constitution with a letter from the alphabet (A to G). Scholars are thus able to track in the text the multiple changes that occurred over the four-year period of the document's creation.

In 1961 two early forms (Forms A and B) of the schema came into existence prior to the council. They were the result of Ottaviani's consultations. A revision (Form C = first schema) was sent to the council fathers in 1962 during the first session. They essentially rejected this schema. Form D (= second schema) emerged from the mixed commission's work with subsequent written recommendations from the council fathers; it was edited and submitted to the council in April 1963, but it was never discussed during the second session of the council. Form E (= third schema, which was the basis for the final schema) was constructed from D on the basis of recommendations submitted to the Theological Commission and its subcommittee from June 1963 to January 1964. This schema was discussed in late September and early October 1964 during the third session of the council, and led to a further revision (Form F = fourth schema), which was discussed in September 1965 during the fourth session of the council. The council fathers made further recommendations for modification that led to Form G (= final schema), which was voted on and basically accepted on October 29, 1965, with minor emendations. Form G is essentially the final text of the constitution promulgated on November 18, 1965.

For convenience, I offer the following chart as a simplified way to track the changed outlines of the three major schemas. Keep in mind the process discussed above. The first schema was the one that the council fathers essentially rejected. The second schema was never discussed in session, but underwent many revisions by means of written suggestions. The final schema began as a third draft but also underwent numerous revisions, as a result both of oral interventions in the aula and written recommendations. Before achieving its final form and title, the document underwent two more revisions.

SCHEMA #1	SCHEMA #2 *never discussed during the 2nd session of the council*	FINAL SCHEMA *(Based essentially on a third schema, but refined in successive revisions)*
Date: November 1962	**Date**: April 1963	**Date**: <u>Adopted November 18, 1965</u>
Title: The Dogmatic Constitution on the Sources of Revelation (*De fontibus revelationis*)	**Title**: On Divine Revelation (*De Divine Revelatione*)	**Title**: The Dogmatic Constitution on Divine Revelation (*Dei Verbum*)
Outline: *G.S. & T* ***Chapter 1.*** The Double Source of <u>Revelation</u> ***Chapter 2.*** The Inspiration, <u>Inerrancy</u>, and Literary Form of Scripture ***Chapter 3.*** The Old Testament ***Chapter 4.*** The New Testament ***Chapter 5.*** Holy Scripture in the Church	**Outline:** *Prologue* ***Chapter 1.*** The Revealed Word of God ***Chapter 2.*** The Divine Inspiration and Interpretation of Sacred Scripture ***Chapter 3.*** The Old Testament ***Chapter 4.*** The New Testament ***Chapter 5.*** The Use of Scripture in the Church	**Outline:** *Preface* ***Chapter 1.*** Revelation Itself ***Chapter 2.*** Handing on Divine <u>Revelation</u> ***Chapter 3.*** Sacred Scripture, Its Inspiration and Divine Interpretation ***Chapter 4.*** The Old Testament ***Chapter 5.*** The New Testament ***Chapter 6.*** Sacred Scripture in the Life of the Church

Comparison of the Main Schemas of *Dei Verbum*

SCHOLARLY INFLUENCES ON THE CONSTITUTION

In recounting this complicated history, we have noted only some of the influences on the final form of the constitution, especially the interventions of some of the council fathers. But I wish to round out our discussion by pointing out the broader scholarly influences that can also be discerned in the final text.

Yves Congar (d. 1995), one of the great theologians of the council and a renowned ecclesiologist, certainly had important influence on the crafting of *Dei Verbum*. Ratzinger himself noted that one could easily "recognize the pen of Y. Congar in the text..." in some sections of the constitution.[38] Congar had written extensively on the area of ecclesiology, and although his work had been viewed suspiciously by some, especially in Rome, his expertise was undeniable. Congar's publications were virtually without parallel, especially in the area of church Tradition, which was one of the thorniest issues discussed in the debates over *Dei Verbum*.[39]

Many other important theologians, most of them *periti* at the council, also had input into the drafting process, especially after the first schema was rejected. The names read like an international who's who of theological experts: Umberto Betti, Lucien Cerfaux, Béda Rigaux, Karl Rahner, Alois Grillmeier, Joseph Ratzinger, Otto Semmelroth, Pieter Smulders, Gérard Philips, Ernst Vogt, and Alexander Kerrigan. Additionally, theologians like Barnabas Ahern, Jean Danielou, Hans Küng, Marie-Dominique Chenu, Luis Alonso-Schökel, and others exercised a great deal of influence on the council by their writings and their availability to the council fathers. Some of them gave regular conferences to the bishops in order to update them on the latest developments in theology and biblical studies.

At one point, while the council fathers were considering the first schema, Yves Congar, Edward Schillebeeckx, and Karl Rahner (d. 1984) circulated among numerous participants at the council their critiques of the first schema as well as their own alternative formulations. Rahner's critique went so far as to call for an entirely new draft, and his observations were instrumental in persuading several American participants to oppose the first draft. Actually, Rahner's participation in the council was itself somewhat of a miracle. He was an extremely well-known theologian who had expected to be invited to the council as a *peritus*. When the Vatican published the list of the 190 invited *periti*, however, Rahner's name was not on it. He had considerable opposition among theologians at the Roman schools, so his name did not find favor among officials at the curia. Cardinal Franz König nevertheless brought him along to be a personal adviser. In the end, his presence was of enormous importance not only for König and the German-speaking bishops but for the council in general.[40]

The point in making these observations is that the production of a major document like *Dei Verbum*, especially at an ecumenical council, is a complex process requiring great expertise. The council fathers alone could never have managed it without professional assistance. There is always a delicate balance between theologians and the magisterium, and I believe the story of *Dei Verbum* illustrates, in part, how the two can cooperate for the benefit of the church. Although one must clearly allow for the influence of the Holy Spirit in this amazing saga, we should never forget the contributions of the faithful theologians and biblical scholars who exercised their professional skills for the good of the church. They, along with the council fathers, deserve credit for having helped shape the constitution.

PART II

Major Points

The Dogmatic Constitution on Divine Revelation, with its twenty-six "articles," is relatively brief, yet comprehensive. It consists of a one-paragraph introductory preface and six chapters, five of which are primarily doctrinal and theological. The sixth and final chapter is devoted to pastoral ramifications of the document's main themes. After presenting the outline of the document, we will summarize the contents of each chapter.

OUTLINE OF *DEI VERBUM*

Preface

Chapter 1. Revelation Itself

Chapter 2. Handing on Divine Revelation

Chapter 3. Sacred Scripture, Its Inspiration
and Divine Interpretation

Chapter 4. The Old Testament

Chapter 5. The New Testament

Chapter 6. Sacred Scripture in the Life of the Church

THE CONSTITUTION AS A WHOLE

Preface

As is customary with many official Vatican documents, the first Latin words give the constitution its title—*Dei verbum* (word of God)—which begins the opening statement, "Hearing the word of God with reverence and proclaiming it with faith...." (*DV*, 1). The preface makes explicit reference to "following in the footsteps of the Council of Trent and of the First Vatican Council." This establishes the primary historical context of the document. It is to be seen in continuity with the magisterial teaching of two of the church's most important councils.

With its explicit mention of the Father, the Son, and the Holy Spirit, the preface also demonstrates the strongly trinitarian orientation of the entire document. Divine revelation is a self-manifestation of a God who is in essence both personal and relational. Especially noteworthy is the poetic quotation from the First Letter of John:

> We declare to you what was from the beginning, what we have heard, what we have seen with our eyes, what we have looked at and touched with our hands, concerning the word of life—this life was revealed, and we have seen it and testify to it, and declare to you the eternal life that was with the Father and was revealed to us—we declare to you what we have seen and heard so that you also may have fellowship with us; and truly our fellowship is with the Father and with his Son Jesus Christ. (1 John 1:1–3)

The quotation sets the tone of the document by referencing the process of communication (announcing the message, the *kerygma*) and speaking explicitly of fellowship with God and one another. Revelation is thus essentially interpersonal.

The text goes on to state the purpose of the document: "to set forth authentic doctrine on divine revelation and how it is handed on" in order to bring all people to faith, hope, and love (*DV*, 1). Understanding divine revelation involves a progression in these three fundamental Christian virtues. Finally, the preface points to an underlying "pastoral" goal, which was uncharacteristic of prior church dogmatic constitutions, but which reflects boldly John XXIII's expressed desire regarding the nature of the council.

Chapter 1: Revelation Itself

This chapter contains five articles (articles 2–6). It includes several scriptural quotations and many citations (e.g., Heb 1:1–2; John 1:1–18), especially from the Pauline letters (Romans, Ephesians, 1–2 Corinthians). The chapter focuses on the nature of divine revelation.

At the outset the constitution emphasizes the personal rather than the propositional dimension of revelation (*DV*, 2 and 6). God is an invisible personal being who reveals himself through "words and deeds" that have an "inner unity" and constitute a divine plan of salvation for all humanity. This explicit mention of words and deeds is a way of acknowledging that revelation takes place in the context of human history into which Jesus Christ himself is born. Revelation is not merely a matter of words but also of deeds. It is both salvific and sacramental. Interestingly, revelation is described as both a plan that is made manifest concretely and a mystery (consistently singular, as in the Pauline corpus, rather than "mysteries," as in prior church documents). Thus, revelation encompasses both knowable and unknowable aspects.

The strong christological dimension of *Dei Verbum*, a crucial and innovative feature of the constitution, is also evident in this section. We would not be exaggerating to say that Christology dominates the entire text. While the constitution mentions the Holy Spirit some twenty-three times, nevertheless Jesus Christ is its centerpiece, precisely because he embodies God's ultimate revelation to the world. Jesus Christ is the Incarnate Word through whom all things are made (John 1:3). He is both "the mediator and the fullness of all revelation" (*DV*, 2). He speaks the words of God and *is* the Word of God. Because he is God's definitive and ultimate revelation to the world, "we now await no further new public revelation" before Jesus' eschatological return in glory (*DV*, 4).

Revelation, the constitution states, is available to all human beings through the light of natural, human reason (*DV*, 6). Creation itself mediates God's message, which is knowable "with ease" and which communicates God's truth "with solid certainty and with no trace of error." Yet achieving the correct understanding of God's plan requires the aid of the Holy Spirit who opens our eyes to God's truth (*DV*, 5). Thus, an equally strong pneumatological emphasis is found in the document, expressed elsewhere by the Holy Spirit's role in the inspiration and enduring truth of Scripture (*DV*, 9 and 11).

The chapter also offers an abridged history of salvation, beginning with "our first parents" (i.e., Adam and Eve) and continuing through

Abraham, the patriarchs, Moses, and the prophets. This abbreviated history of salvation culminates in Jesus Christ, who brings the "new and definitive covenant" of God with humanity.

Chapter 2: Handing on Divine Revelation

Having described revelation in general terms in chapter 1, the constitution now turns to the *process* of revelation, i.e., the complex issue of *how* this divine revelation takes place. This chapter contains only four numbered articles (*DV*, 7–10), but they are densely packed with important assertions.

The chapter begins with reference again to Christ the Lord as the epitome of God's self-revelation. But it quickly draws attention to the apostolic preaching of the followers of Jesus. Revelation is rooted in the oral proclamation (i.e., preaching; Greek, *kerygma*) of the apostles and proceeds, under the guidance and inspiration of the Holy Spirit, to be committed to writing. The notion of divine inspiration fills this chapter, yet nowhere does the constitution describe or define inspiration in explicit terms. Instead, the text affirms that God's inspiration of the Scriptures guarantees their fidelity to the message of salvation contained in them.

Simultaneously, these articles affirm that the process of "handing on" God's revelation allows for development in the understanding of these truths (*DV*, 8), yet constitutes a "deposit" that accompanies the "pilgrim Church" on its journey of faith (cf. *DV*, 7 and *LG*, 48). In its teaching, life, and worship the church faithfully passes on the essence of this revelation to all future generations (*DV*, 8). There is a certain tension within the document at this point between the more personal and dynamic aspect of revelation (e.g., the "living tradition" in article 8) and the more traditional, static, and propositional dimension of revelation (e.g., "deposit" in article 10).

Articles 9 and 10 are particularly critical to this chapter. They discuss the complex relationship between Scripture and Tradition, which must be considered one of the most important aspects of the constitution. We will return to this topic later, but briefly these articles set forth the main components of the interrelationship between Scripture and Tradition:

- Both flow from the same "divine wellspring" of truth.

- Both constitute inspired revelation under the guidance of the Holy Spirit.

- They are not two separate sources but "one sacred deposit of the Word of God."

- The teaching office of the church authoritatively interprets Sacred Scripture yet it "is not above the Word of God, but serves it...."

Interestingly, after these two interrelated dimensions of revelation (Scripture and Tradition) have been clearly laid out, the final article uses an expression that seemingly adds a third element, namely, the "teaching authority of the church" (article 10, *ecclesiae magisterium*), as if it were distinct from both the Word of God and the living Tradition of the church. This is a subtle indication that the notion of Tradition is not limited to the official teaching of the church but is a broader concept. Unfortunately, the constitution never clarifies precisely how the magisterium relates to both Scripture and Tradition.

Throughout this section of the constitution one can discern a tendency to embrace "both/and" aspects of the Catholic faith, e.g., Scripture *and* Tradition, Word *and* sacrament, personal *and* propositional aspects of revelation.

Chapter 3: Sacred Scripture, Its Inspiration and Divine Interpretation

This chapter, containing three articles (*DV*, 11–13), is deceptively short. In attempting to explain the complex process of divine inspiration, it maintains a careful balance between the divine and human origins of the Scriptures. I summarize the main points as follows:

- God is the "author" of the Scriptures, but the human writers are also "true authors" who communicated faithfully God's intended message.

- No specific theory of inspiration is adopted, but several biblical passages that affirm the inspired nature of both

Testaments are cited (i.e., John 20:31; 2 Tim 3:16; 2 Pet 1:19–20; 3:15–16).

- The Scriptures communicate the divine message in human language; thus, any interpreter must consider the literary forms and conventions of communication of biblical times (e.g., words, style, customs) in order to interpret the message accurately.

- The Scriptures communicate "faithfully and without error that truth which God put into sacred writings for the sake of salvation."

- The Scriptures have an inherent unity in them that must influence their authentic interpretation.

There are three things worth noting here. First, background for the exhortation in article 12 to biblical interpreters to pay attention to literary forms in the Scriptures is seen in Pius XII's historic encyclical *Divino Afflante Spiritu*, which is footnoted. This is implicit confirmation of the importance of modern, scientific study of the Bible.

Second, article 12 emphasizes the necessity of interpreting Scripture in its broader context that reflects the "content and unity" of the entire sacred canon. The constitution also explains how scriptural interpretation must always respect "the living Tradition of the whole Church", because of the unity that exists in the faith. Interpretation from a Catholic perspective is thus always in this broader context.

Third, the final sentence of article 13 is striking in its comparison of the dual human/divine nature of Scripture with the same dual nature of Jesus Christ:

> For the words of God expressed in human language have been made like human discourse, just as the Word of the eternal Father, when he took to himself the flesh of human weakness, was in every way made like men. (*DV*, 13)

This statement underlines the unfathomable way in which divine revelation works. It is ultimately a mystery of "incarnation" that brings the human and divine together to communicate one coherent message.

[handwritten: divine plan of salvation for all humanity.]

Chapter 4: The Old Testament

This chapter (*DV*, 14–16), along with the following one, is descriptive in nature and at face value seems to contain no real surprises. Yet its inclusion at all is important because it affirms the enduring value of this Testament in its own right. The constitution expresses the traditional view of the Old Testament as "permanently valuable" and just as important as the New Testament, in one sense, because it is divinely inspired and contains "the true Word of God" (*DV*, 14). The Old Testament, in fact, lays out the divine plan of salvation for all humanity. Chapter 4 telescopes this plan into a kind of shorthand, noting only the covenants with Abraham and Moses, and pointing out the contribution of the prophets.

[handwritten margin note: Old It same value New]

Also in line with earlier church tradition is the chapter's description of the dialectical relationship of the Old and New Testaments. The New Testament is "hidden" in the Old, while the Old is "made manifest" in the New (*DV*, 16). The text affirms that, from a Christian perspective, the Old Testament, while it contains an authentic record of God's revelation to humankind, is always "incomplete and temporary" (*DV*, 15). The Old Testament thus has limitations. Christians honor and revere these books because they contain "true divine pedagogy," but the fullness of their meaning can be found only in the New Testament.[1]

[handwritten: The New Testament is "hidden" in the Old, while the Old is "made manifest" in the New.]

Chapter 5: The New Testament

[handwritten: → venta—]

This chapter (*DV*, 17–20) highlights the divine inspiration of the New Testament books and emphasizes, along with ancient church tradition, the special place of the four canonical Gospels. The doctrine of the Incarnation stands out in this section. It is mentioned twice, especially in connection with the "deeds and words" of Jesus Christ who himself is the incarnate Word. This explicit phrasing harks back to article 2 of the document, where revelation is described as God's deeds and words wrought throughout human history. The Gospels give witness to the incarnate Word; thus, special attention must be given them.

Article 19 is crucial in this chapter. It is also one of the most controversial sections of the constitution, for it demonstrates quite clearly the compromises that were made during the council. This article affirms

The background of Article 19 the PBC's 1964 Doc

the basic historicity of the Gospels yet acknowledges the multiple layers of tradition that they contain and the complicated process by which the evangelists formed the Gospels. The background of this article is the PBC's 1964 document *Sancta Mater Ecclesia* ("The Historical Truth of the Gospels").[2] In fact, we should note that the very words "Holy Mother Church" (*Sancta Mater Ecclesia*) begin article 19, a direct allusion to the PBC's document.

According to the PBC instruction, three layers of tradition must be acknowledged in the Gospels: oral, written, and edited. The constitution subtly adopts this outline with the following words:

> The sacred authors wrote the four Gospels, selecting some things from the many which had been handed on by word of mouth or in writing, reducing some of them to a synthesis, explaining some things in view of the situation of their churches, and preserving the form of proclamation, but always in such fashion that they told us the honest truth about Jesus. For their intention in writing was that either from their own memory and recollections or from the witness of those who "themselves from the beginning were eyewitnesses and ministers of the Word," we might know "the truth" concerning those matters about which we have been instructed (cf. Luke 1:2-4). (*DV*, 19)

Admitting that the evangelists selected some of the traditions about Jesus, "reducing some of them to a synthesis" and explaining them "in view of the situation of their churches" assumes that the Gospels are not always literally historical, although they tell us "the honest truth about Jesus." This back and forth dialectic in the article is a result of the tensions among the council fathers, some of whom wanted to emphasize literal historicity in the Bible, while others wanted to emphasize the results of historical-critical methods of study that pointed to a broader concept of the "truth" of the Gospels.

Chapter 6: Sacred Scripture in the Life of the Church

The final chapter, with its six articles (*DV*, 21–26), contains both new and old insights. It is the only chapter devoted to the pastoral ramifications of the church's teaching on divine revelation. Some might consequently dismiss it as doctrinally insignificant, but one prominent Protestant observer at the council called it "a key for the understanding of the whole Constitution."[3] Indeed, it prominently reiterates the crucial relationship between Sacred Scripture and Tradition, insisting that they are one unified source of revelation, not two (*DV*, 24).

The chapter's first line is most striking:

> The Church has always venerated the divine Scriptures just as she venerates the body of the Lord, since, especially in the sacred liturgy, she unceasingly receives and offers to the faithful the bread of life from the table both of God's word and of Christ's body. (*DV*, 21)

This virtual equation of Sacred Scripture with the Eucharist, which is described elsewhere as "the source and summit of the Christian faith" (*LG*, 11; see *CCC*, 1324 and *SC*, 10), is remarkable for its attribution of divine presence to these two different modes. This perspective is consistent with Vatican II's teaching on the liturgy, which also emphasizes that the risen Christ is present as much in the Word as in the eucharistic species of consecrated bread and wine (*SC*, 7).[4]

The explicitly pastoral nature of this chapter is apparent in several ways.

- The Scriptures are described as "food for the soul, the pure and everlasting source of spiritual life" (article 21).

- All liturgical preaching should be "nourished and regulated by Sacred Scripture," for liturgical preaching "must hold the foremost place" in the church's ministry of the Word (articles 21 and 24).

- All Christian faithful should have easy access to Scripture in good and reliable vernacular translations (article 22) and should be encouraged to read the Bible in order to better know Christ (article 25).

- Among historical translations of the Bible, the Greek Septuagint and the Latin Vulgate hold a special place of honor (article 22).

- In keeping with the ecumenical nature of the council, modern translations, where possible, should be produced "in cooperation with the separated brethren" for the benefit of all (articles 23 and 25).

- Priests, deacons, and catechists have special responsibility to be informed about Scripture, utilizing the means of liturgy, devotional reading, instruction, and prayer (article 25).

- Catholic exegetes and biblical scholars are encouraged to do their professional work, recognizing also the legitimate oversight provided by apostolic authorities in the church (the pope and bishops) (article 23).

This chapter contains a noteworthy expression, rooted in two prior papal encyclicals, that has captured the imagination of successive generations of Catholics: "...the study of the sacred page is, as it were, the soul of sacred theology" (*DV*, 24). The importance of the Word of God for theology is thus underscored, but in a way that also preserves the role of church Tradition in theology (*DV*, 24). In the conclusion of the constitution, its pastoral orientation dovetails with its doctrinal teaching to inform the life of the church and strengthen the faith of all believers. As in the opening article, the constitution closes with direct quotations from Sacred Scripture (2 Thess 3:1; Isa 40:8; 1 Pet 1:23–25), expressing the desired goal of having the eternal Word of God spread rapidly throughout the world (*DV*, 26).

Sources in the Constitution

The constitution employs a wide variety of biblical citations from both the Old and New Testaments, with quotations or allusions from Paul's letters appearing prominently. There are seventy-four scriptural references in the main text and many more in the footnotes. The document also cites numerous patristic sources (i.e., Augustine, Jerome, Irenaeus, John Chrysostom, Cyril of Jerusalem, Theodore of Mopsuestia, Cyprian, and Ambrose). Quotations from the Councils of Trent and Vatican I, as well as Nicaea II and the Fourth Council of

Constance, are also utilized on occasion, indicating some continuity with declarations from prior church councils. Pertinent papal encyclicals from Leo XIII, Benedict XV, Pius XI, and Pius XII are quoted as well. Interestingly, the PBC's document *Sancta Mater Ecclesia* is cited explicitly only once (in article 19), although its influence is apparent in several passages.

MAJOR EMPHASES, CONTINUITY, AND NOVELTY

Before proceeding to describe emphases in detail, a comparison of *Dei Verbum* with the church's two previous major teaching documents on divine revelation is instructive. The chart on the facing page allows us to see quickly the primary divergences.

This schematic outline shows that *Dei Verbum* was indeed a different breed of constitution. First, it contained a fully developed treatment of the subject, a treatment that was independent and not part of a larger topic. Second, it attempted to address multiple, complex aspects of the topic, with an eye toward unity in its approach. Finally, the absence of condemnations (anathemas) is noticeable. The tone is thus less defensive and confrontational than either Trent or Vatican I. In fact, in comparison to previous councils in the church's history, Vatican II is noteworthy for the absence of *any* condemnation, which is a remarkable testimony to its positive outreach to other Christians and to the world at large. *Dei Verbum*'s ecumenical spirit is just one of the features of the constitution that make it so singularly different from its predecessors.

Yet we would exaggerate if we were to say that *Dei Verbum* totally broke the mold of the church's teaching on revelation. On the contrary, much of its content is in direct continuity with traditional Catholic teaching on revelation and the Bible. To list just a few of these areas:

- Revelation is ultimately a mystery of how God relates to human beings.

- God is known in the doctrine of the Trinity, the understanding that God is mysteriously three persons and yet one.

TRENT	VATICAN I	VATICAN II
Fourth Session, 1546	Third Session, 1870	Fourth Session, 1965
Title: No formal title, but concerned acceptance of the sacred books and apostolic traditions, the role of the Latin Vulgate, and means of interpretation	**Title**: "On Revelation"	**Title**: "Dogmatic Constitution on Divine Revelation"
Content: Revelation is not discussed as a separate topic; rather, two decrees set forth the following: • the definitive canon of Sacred Scripture for the church (46 books in the Old Testament; 27 books in the New Testament) • the priority of the Latin Vulgate; • the affirmation that God is the author of both Testaments, either by the preaching of Christ or the dictation of the Holy Spirit; • an emphasis on the church's definitive role in interpreting the Scriptures and forbidding individual interpretation Anathemas and restrictions placed within the context of the two decrees, including restricting what biblical texts, with notes and/or interpretations, printers may print	**Content:** Revelation is discussed in chapter 2 of the Dogmatic Constitution on the Catholic Faith, most of which reiterates the basic teaching on Scripture from the Council of Trent

보충 설명

Supplemented by four anathemas: 파요
1. Against those who deny that God can be known through human reason and the created order
2. Against those who deny the necessity of learning about God and the importance of worshiping
3. Against those who affirm human self-development rather than acknowledging that God elevates human beings to divine perfection
4. Against those who deny the canonical authority of all the books of the Old and New Testament | **Content:** A dogmatic constitution fully devoted to the topic of divine revelation, discussed in an introduction and six chapters, covering the topics of revelation itself, the transmission of revelation, the divine inspiration of Scripture, the interrelationship of the Old and New Testaments, and the pastoral role of the Scriptures in the life of the church

No anathemas |

Comparison of Trent, Vatican I, and Vatican II on Revelation

- Jesus Christ is the ultimate revelation of God, the new and eternal covenant.

- The Holy Spirit is the chief interpreter of Scriptures and is the faithful guarantor of the faith of the church.

- God can be known through different means in revelation, including creation itself, the Scriptures, and church teaching.

- Sacred Scripture is God's Word in human words; the Bible communicates faithfully and without error God's sacred message.

- The Holy Spirit inspired Sacred Scripture.

- The church has the right and duty to be the final arbiter of the meaning of the Sacred Scriptures.

- Sacred Scripture alone does not contain the whole of revelation nor is it solely sufficient for living a faithful Christian life; church Tradition must also be honored.

- The Septuagint, the Vulgate, and the patristic commentators hold a time-honored place in the history of interpretation.

- The Scriptures have multiple layers of meaning that come to life in different eras of the church's life.

My point is that such ideas in *Dei Verbum*, among others, are quite consistent with prior church teaching, even if their expression in the document is at times nuanced in a different fashion. But there are elements in *Dei Verbum* that are quite novel. Some of them were the product of intense debate before they were incorporated into the final text.[5] I will list twenty-one observations about major emphases in the document, some of which express continuity and others novelty.

1. God's self-revelation to human beings lies at the heart of Catholic and Christian theology. The constitution expresses itself in ways that are essentially consistent with the church's standard teaching on this doctrine. God freely chooses to reveal himself and his will through

various means. Jesus Christ is God's ultimate revelation to the world, and he is therefore the focal point for all discussion of revelation.

Dei Verbum, however, uses a different way of expressing this doctrine. The constitution expresses a *personalist* view of revelation. Rather than using the static and philosophical language of earlier church declarations, *Dei Verbum* speaks in more personal tones influenced by biblical concepts. The council fathers clearly rejected a traditional *propositional* view of revelation, whereby the emphasis is given to the set of dogmas and doctrines that constitute authentic "church teaching." Instead, the document emphasizes revelation as the act of a trinitarian God whose very nature is self-giving. God's self-revelation initates a dialogue between God and humankind. God invites people into relationship, and we are asked to respond. God speaks to us as "friends"; we are "to share in the divine nature" (*DV*, 2).

2. Just as important is the emphasis on the unity of "words and deeds" in the process of revelation (*DV*, 2). This expression squarely places revelation in the context of human history. Whereas prior church teaching had placed primary emphasis on revelation as "word" (i.e., Scripture), this constitution affirms the unity of God's words and deeds in the course of salvation history, emphasizing the unified, sacramental aspect of God's revelation. God is thus knowable in multiple and varied ways. God is revealed in creation itself, in the history of Israel, in the history of the church, and especially in the person, life, death, and resurrection of Jesus Christ. Human reason is able to reckon with this divine revelation, since God does not communicate in ways totally immune to human perception.

3. Although *Dei Verbum* affirms that Christ is the ultimate revelation (*DV*, 4), there is a sense of openness to the fact that our understanding of revelation continues to grow in every era.

> For there is a growth in the understanding of the realities and the words which have been handed down.... For as the centuries succeed one another, the Church constantly moves

forward toward the fullness of divine truth until the words of
God reach their complete fulfillment in her. (*DV*, 8)

Thus, *Dei Verbum* contains a more dynamic view of revelation than
previous teachings. Its emphasis on the "living tradition" and "living
teaching office" of the church (*DV*, 8 and 10) is rather novel, and to
some, a daunting notion. Unlike earlier teachings on revelation, *Dei
Verbum* does not relegate revelation simply to the past. Although it
never clarifies with precision how or to what extent development of
doctrine takes place, it nonetheless refuses to limit revelation to past
events or to the Scriptures alone. *Dei Verbum* goes so far as to admit of
"a growth in the understanding of the realities and the words" that
have been handed down (*DV*, 8). This remarkable approach is distinctive in comparison to prior church teaching on revelation, as at Vatican I, which tended to emphasize the static nature of revelation as
permanent and unchanging.

4. The constitution also employs the language of a "pilgrim Church"
(*DV*, 7; see also *LG*, 48), a notion that has become commonplace in
the post–Vatican II era as evidence of the church's permanent evolution on its way to the kingdom of God. This notion reinforces the
conviction of the constitution that revelation is not a static reality. The
church itself must grow and evolve as time goes on, interacting with
the truth revealed by God and continually trying to deepen its understanding of that truth.

5. When speaking of sacred Tradition and both Testaments as a "mirror" (*DV*, 7 *speculum*), the constitution surprisingly prefigures later
methodological developments in biblical studies. Starting in the early
1980s especially, newer approaches to critical study of the Bible began
to put less emphasis on the "historical" dimensions of the Scriptures—in
which they were viewed as "windows" into the past—and began instead
to see the Scriptures more as "mirrors" that reflect back to us what we
are and are called to be. Revelation is God's mirror that reveals to us our
true identity and goal, namely, to be members of the kingdom of God
where we will see God face to face (cf. 1 Cor 13:12; 1 John 3:2).

6. Not only does revelation testify to God's free sharing of himself with humankind, but revelation gives people a firm sense of God's will and a vision of God's wisdom. Quoting in part Vatican I, the document says:

> Through divine revelation, God chose to show forth and communicate Himself and the eternal decisions of His will regarding the salvation of men. That is to say, He chose to share with them those divine treasures which totally transcend the understanding of the human mind.

This wisdom is particularly found in the proclamation of the Gospel of Jesus Christ, which communicates what is necessary for "all saving truth and moral teaching" (*DV*, 2).

7. Throughout the document there is an emphasis on continuity in the process of revelation. While not a new concept, this continuity is expressed in several ways. Continuity can be seen as existing in church teaching itself. *Dei Verbum* is replete with quotations both from Sacred Scripture and from prior church teachings, especially the Council of Trent and Vatican I. In addition, the insistence that there is only one source of revelation, although expressed in both Scripture and Tradition, emphasizes the unity of God's will being revealed in different ways. Continuity is also found in the concept of apostolic succession, whereby the bishops as successors of the apostles are guarantors of the fidelity of the tradition (*DV*, 7 and 8). There is a direct movement, according to *Dei Verbum*, from the apostles to the bishops in order to protect the authenticity of the faith. Finally, another source of continuity is found in the Bible itself. The Old Testament and the New Testament relate to one another intimately and testify unanimously to the one revelation of the God who animates them both.

8. Consistent with much church teaching prior to the twentieth century, *Dei Verbum* emphasizes the unique authoritative role that the church has in the process of revelation. The magisterium of the church, under the direct guidance of the Holy Spirit, guarantees the authenticity of

the truth it proclaims. The document goes to considerable lengths to affirm this, yet it also acknowledges that the teaching office serves the truth.

> But the task of authentically interpreting the word of God, whether written or handed on, has been entrusted exclusively to the living teaching office of the Church whose authority is exercised in the name of Jesus Christ. This teaching office is not above the word of God, but serves it, teaching only what has been handed on, listening to it devoutly, guarding it scrupulously and explaining it faithfully in accord with a divine commission and with the help of the Holy Spirit.... (*DV*, 10)

Scripture & Tradition

9. Probably the most prominent theme in *Dei Verbum* is the elusive relationship between Scripture and Tradition (especially in articles 9 and 10). We shall return to this topic at length in Part Three. Suffice it to say here that the document's bold statement that Scripture and Tradition constitute one unified source of revelation was both controversial and an advance beyond prior church teachings. The concept was made even more complex by mention of the magisterium of the church, which seems to constitute an intimately related yet distinctive reality.

> It is clear, therefore, that sacred tradition, Sacred Scripture and the teaching authority (*ecclesiae magisterium*) of the Church, in accord with God's most wise design, are so linked and joined together that one cannot stand without the others, and that all together and each in its own way under the action of the one Holy Spirit contribute effectively to the salvation of souls. (*DV*, 10)

NEW

This unity of revelation, expressed in the complex terms of Scripture, Tradition, and the magisterium, constitutes a new direction at Vatican II.

We should also point out here that, unlike prior church teachings (e.g., at Trent), *Dei Verbum* does not use the plural word "traditions" but always the singular "Tradition." (The one exception to this rule is in article 8, where the plural form occurs because of a citation from

Question? traditions vs Tradition

Scripture [2 Thess 2:15].) Emphasis is thus on the breadth and unity of church Tradition rather than an accumulation of ancient practices or teachings.

10. As one would expect, a prominent theme is the concept of inspiration that infuses revelation. *Dei Verbum* affirms the doctrine of inspiration, namely, that God is the ultimate author of Sacred Scripture and the Holy Spirit is the faithful guide of the human authors of the Scriptures. As the text explicitly states:

> …the books of both the Old and New Testaments in their entirety, with all their parts, are sacred and canonical because written under the inspiration of the Holy Spirit, they have God as their author…. (*DV*, 11)

One should note that the document does not adopt a specific explanation of how inspiration works (i.e., verbal inspiration, authorial inspiration, and so on). Rather, it affirms inspiration in a broad fashion.

11. As a corollary to this, the document also affirms that "the books of Scripture must be acknowledged as teaching solidly, faithfully and without error that truth which God wanted put into sacred writings for the sake of salvation" (*DV*, 11). This statement seems consistent with prior church teaching until one realizes that the council fathers avoided using a strict description of "verbal inerrancy" in favor of a broader expression regarding the truth that is necessary for salvation. That is, the text uses the phrase "without error" (*sine errore*) and not the term "inerrant," which is identified with literal verbal inerrancy. This formulation keeps the Catholic Church out of the orbit of a fundamentalist approach to inspiration and biblical inerrancy, which actually was more characteristic of earlier church teaching, even in Leo XIII's enlightened *Providentissimus Deus* (articles 20 and 21).

12. Coupled with the theme above is an emphasis on the human dimension of producing the Sacred Scriptures. Not only is there

explicit acknowledgment of the need to pay attention to literary forms and other influences on literary expression in the original biblical languages, but it is stated that the goal of interpretation is to uncover "the intention of the sacred writers" (*DV*, 12). The document goes on to say that

> since God speaks in Sacred Scripture through men in human fashion, the interpreter of Sacred Scripture, in order to see clearly what God wanted to communicate to us, should carefully investigate what meaning the sacred writers really intended, and what God wanted to manifest by means of their words. (*DV*, 12)

Incarnational principle

13. Another emphasis in *Dei Verbum* might be called its incarnational principle. In various ways the document affirms the basic truth that God gets involved directly in human affairs. The primary means, of course, is the Incarnation of Christ himself. He constitutes the ultimate revelation in human flesh of the eternal Godhead who draws near to his beloved people. The document makes an explicit comparison between this truth of the Incarnation and the Sacred Scriptures:

> For the words of God, expressed in human language, have been made like human discourse, just as the word of the eternal Father, when He took to Himself the flesh of human weakness, was in every way made like men. (*DV*, 13)

A further connection with the incarnational principle is the comparison of the sacred writings with the Eucharist. Just as the sacraments are concrete signs of God's grace at work in our world and our lives, so the Word of God is a concrete sign of God's presence.

> The Church has always venerated the divine Scriptures just as she venerates the body of the Lord, since, especially in the sacred liturgy, she unceasingly receives and offers to the faithful the bread of life from the table both of God's word and of Christ's body. (*DV*, 21)

modern, scientific tools.

14. Underlying much of the document implicitly, but never expressed explicitly, is the tacit assumption that the church must approach the Scriptures with the modern, scientific tools that are the basis of sound biblical exegesis. The document encourages Catholic biblical scholars to make faithful translations of the Bible from the original languages (*DV*, 22) and to go about their work of interpretation faithfully (*DV*, 23). The text also reminds everyone that "the study of the sacred page is, as it were, the soul of sacred theology" (*DV*, 24). This expression, which comes from *Providentissmus Deus*, has inspired theologians since Vatican II to utilize the Word of God profoundly in all their expertise in the performance of their craft. Furthermore, explicit mention of the "apostolic preaching" that underlies the Gospels (*DV*, 18), and the selecting, synthesizing, and explaining conducted by the biblical authors (*DV*, 19), is a subtle way of referring to the exercise of form and redaction criticism, two of the scientific methods of biblical study used in the nineteenth and twentieth centuries. All of this assumes that Catholic scholars will exercise their duties utilizing whatever tools are available to make the understanding of God's Word available to a wide audience.

15. Especially in chapters 4 and 5 of the document, the symbiotic relationship between the Old and New Testaments is a major theme. These chapters are primarily descriptive in nature, but there is a fundamental teaching contained in them. Both Testaments were formed under the guidance of the one and same Holy Spirit. Both constitute the Word of God. The Old Testament continues to have its own validity, although its true goal is to prepare for the fuller revelation found in the New Testament. The New Testament fulfills the vision of the Old Testament and displays that Testament's most profound meaning (*DV*, 15). Preeminent in the New Testament are the four canonical Gospels, because they recount the life of the Savior.

Yet there is something novel in the constitution's teaching on the Old Testament. The devotion of an entire chapter, even though rather short, to the Old Testament is important. Although the expression of the interrelationship of the two testaments is traditional, the great encyclicals of Leo XIII and Pius XII, for instance, did not address the validity of the Old Testament in its own right.

16. One consistent aspect of *Dei Verbum* that is in harmony with prior church teachings on revelation is the honoring of certain ancient traditions that continue to impact on how revelation is to be understood. In particular, reference is made to the writings of the early church fathers (both from the Eastern and the Western traditions), the prominence of the Septuagint (the Greek translation of the Hebrew Bible), and the Vulgate (St. Jerome's Latin translation of the Bible from the original languages) (*DV*, 22).

17. Something quite new in *Dei Verbum* is the encouragement of an ecumenical approach to biblical translation and dissemination (*DV*, 23). Although this is not a forceful statement, the fact that it is mentioned at all in the final chapter on the pastoral application of the church's teaching is novel and very important.[6] This may well be because the intention of the council was specifically ecumenical. Moreover, Augustin Bea, a biblical scholar and prefect of the Secretariat for Christian Unity, was instrumental in formulating the document. The constitution allows for the possibility both of cooperation with biblical scholars of other denominations to produce viable modern translations (*DV*, 22) and of publishing translations that would have broad ecumenical appeal (*DV*, 25). Even more astounding is that it proposes the development of Bible editions with appropriate explanations that might be useful for non-Christians (*DV*, 26).

18. Another striking emphasis in *Dei Verbum* is the incorporation into the text of the final chapter on the pastoral application of Sacred Scripture in the life of the church. The explicit encouragement of Catholics and indeed all Christians to become familiar with the Bible is new.

> Easy access to Sacred Scripture should be provided for all the Christian faithful. (*DV*, 22)

Prior to Vatican II, Catholics had been warned away from reading the Bible on their own. There was a fear that misinterpretation could too easily take place if people were to read the text on their own. Catholic emphasis was on listening to the official teaching of the church and the preaching of bishops and priests to glean what the Bible taught.

19. In line with the constitution's pastoral intent, the emphasis on the centrality of the "liturgical homily" shows the dramatic shift that took place in the Roman Catholic Church at the time of the council (*DV*, 21 and 24; cf. *SC*, 52). Pre–Vatican II liturgy focused much more on the importance of the moment of consecration of the bread and wine into the body and blood of Christ. Preaching was not a priority, nor was familiarity with the Scriptures. Also, the document's descriptions of the Bible as "food of the soul" and "source of everlasting life" (*DV*, 21) highlight the importance of the Word of God in Catholic life and worship. The document also employs the famous quotation from St. Jerome, "Ignorance of the Scriptures is ignorance of Christ" (*DV*, 25). Moreover, the document urges priests, deacons, and catechists, who are most explicitly charged with disseminating the Word of God by preaching or teaching, to become familiar with the Word and to listen to it carefully for themselves (*DV*, 25). This manifested a significant shift in Catholic practice consistent with the spirit of the reform of the liturgy expressed in *Sacrosanctum Concilium*.

20. *Dei Verbum* also invokes the word "mystery" (singular, as pointed out above) five times in various contexts. It refers to the revealed words in Scripture as clarifying the mystery of God's saving deeds (*DV*, 2), the "mystery of salvation" partly revealed in the Old Testament (*DV*, 15), the mystery of Christ's death, resurrection, and ascension and their salvific significance (*DV*, 17), the mystery of Christ (*DV*, 25), and the mystery of the Eucharist (*DV*, 26). These references overlap to some degree because they all touch on the essential "mystery" of how Jesus Christ reveals God to the world and to the church. Not only does this language place the constitution more in harmony with the biblical notion of the "mystery" of God's plan (e.g., especially in the Pauline letters, such as Rom 16:15; Eph 1:9; 3:3–5, 9; Col 1:26–27), but it also reinforces the notion that we can never ultimately understand every aspect of God's self-revelation here on earth. The constitution uses the word not as a cop-out but as a true signifier

of the profound depth of God's self-revelation at the heart of the message of Sacred Scripture.

21. Finally, although this is more difficult to pinpoint, many interpreters of *Dei Verbum* sense a different tone in the constitution, in comparison to earlier church teachings. It is more even-handed, less polemical, and broader in its outlook. Much of its language is biblical in nature, and it uses biblical quotations liberally (especially from the writings of John and Paul), albeit in a fashion that seems less "proof texting" than earlier church declarations (e.g., *Providentissimus Deus*, 17). The text has no hints of paternalism in it. Rather, there is a profound equation of the presence of Christ in the Word on par with the presence of Christ in the sacraments, especially the Eucharist. The constitution's pastoral and ecumenical orientation has served it well in directing the life of the church in the more than forty years since its promulgation.

While these twenty-one major points do not summarize all that *Dei Verbum* says, they constitute a reasonable listing of the teachings of the document that have had and continue to have a major impact on the life of the church.

COMPROMISE AND INCOMPLETION

All this being said, one can also ask in what ways *Dei Verbum* was a compromise document. It was the product of an intense battle. Sides lined up and argued strongly for their respective positions. As Joseph Ratzinger, then a brilliant young German theologian who served as a council *peritus*, put it:

> The text . . . reveals traces of its difficult history; it is the result of many compromises. But the fundamental compromise which pervades it is more than a compromise, it is a synthesis of great importance. The text combines fidelity to Church tradition with an affirmation of critical scholarship, thus opening up anew the path that faith may follow into the world of today.

It does not entirely abandon the position of Trent and Vatican I, but neither does it mummify what was held to be true at those Councils, because it realizes that fidelity in the sphere of the Spirit can be realized only through a constantly renewed appropriation. With regard to its total achievement, one can say unhesitatingly that the labour of the four-year long controversy was not in vain.[7]

Evidence of compromise in *Dei Verbum* is found in several locations. Three major examples will suffice.

First, there is a tension in the document between the *personalist* and *propositional* views of revelation. The personalist view is emphasized in the sections that speak of God's revelation of himself in words and deeds and primarily in the person of Jesus Christ (*DV*, 2, 4, and 6). This is accompanied elsewhere by language, rooted in late New Testament documents like the pastoral epistles (e.g., 1 Tim 6:20), that speaks of the one "deposit" of faith found in Scripture and Tradition and tied to the teaching office of the church (*DV*, 10). These are not contradictory ideas, but they admit a certain tension between the process of self-revelation and the content of that revelation through history.

Second, the constitution simultaneously upholds the notion that the Scriptures are "without error" (*DV*, 11) and yet implies, by its use of *Sancta Mater Ecclesia*, that the very lengthy and complex process of the formation of the Scriptures (even the Gospels) can allow for accretions and changes in the transmission of the text (*DV*, 20). Moreover, it upholds the basic historicity of the Gospels (*DV*, 19 and 20) while acknowledging that exegetes must carefully pay attention to literary genres, styles of writing, and customs in order to understand what the text says (*DV*, 12).

This section involved (and still does!) much controversy. What exactly is meant by the statement: "... the books of Scripture must be acknowledged as teaching solidly, faithfully and without error (*fideliter et sine errore*) that truth which God wanted put into sacred writings for the sake of salvation (*nostrae salutis causa*)" (*DV*, 11)?[8] Most interpreters note that this view of inspiration places the divine message within the context of soteriology (i.e., the doctrine of salvation). Thus the Scriptures clearly do not err on teachings necessary for salvation (e.g., faith and morals), yet there seems to be some wiggle room for historical or scientific errors in the Scriptures. Indeed, one of the early opponents to the first schema, Cardinal Franz König of Vienna, while addressing the council on the third schema, pointedly reminded the council fathers of various historical errors that are in the Bible (Mark 2:26 where the high priest is misidentified [cf. 1 Sam 21:2]; Matt 27:9, where a quotation is wrongly ascribed; and Dan 1:1, where a wrong date is given for the siege of Jerusalem). Yet the presence of some historical or scientific errors does not undermine the authoritative quality of the whole inspired text.[9]

We should emphasize that the constitution does not lend itself to an interpretation of divided inspiration, as if only the part of Scripture essential to salvation is inspired while other parts are not inspired. The Holy Spirit inspires the whole of Scripture. Yet as Barnabas Ahern, an American biblical scholar and an important *peritus* at the council, stated, in settling on the compromise text, the council fathers rejected an absolutist, fundamentalist doctrine of inerrancy.[10]

Third, not surprisingly, an evolving or developmental notion of Tradition was controversial (*DV*, 8: *traditionis vivificam*). As Joseph Ratzinger points out, however, the controversy came from both sides of the issue.[11] Representing the standard view was Cardinal Ernesto Ruffini of Palermo (Italy). He opposed the idea of an evolving Tradition on the basis of the teaching of the Council of Trent and Vatican I and their insistence on the permanent, unchanging nature of revelation, which concluded with the death of the apostles. From an entirely different perspective, Cardinal Paul Léger of Montreal (Canada) opposed the developmental idea of Tradition because he feared it would interfere with ecumenical discussions with Protestants who, for their own reasons, favored a notion of a limited divine revelation expressed solely in the Bible. This is one instance in the council's history in which elements of both the conservative and progressive wings of the church wanted a similar resolution, albeit for differing reasons. Thus, the challenge for the council fathers was to find language that respected both the unchanging and yet evolving notions of divine revelation. While the truth does not change, the understanding or expression of that truth can indeed change. Both aspects are found in the final text, which preserves the unified contributions of Scripture and Tradition to the life of the church.

These are just a few examples of the kinds of debates that led to compromises in the constitution. In addition to containing compromises, *Dei Verbum* also leaves some questions without complete answers. For example, although it asserts the doctrine of inspiration of the Scriptures, it does not describe how inspiration works. How do the divine author and the human authors interact in such a way that both are true authors? How does the Holy Spirit operate in this process? How does the Bible respect human literary qualities while embodying the divine message? These are the kinds of issues about inspiration that the constitution leaves open-ended.[12]

Even more crucial is the unresolved explanation of the relationship between Scripture and Tradition, which we will discuss in Part Three. Just how does biblical exegesis influence the church's teachings and the formulation of doctrine? Conversely, how does the church's magisterial teaching orient people toward an authentic understanding of the sacred texts? How do we keep in appropriate balance the influence of one upon the other? These issues are not resolved in the text.

Another area the constitution does not tackle is the relationship between the magisterium on one side and theologians and biblical scholars on the other. This relationship has had its ups and downs over the centuries. The constitution is clear that the magisterium retains for itself the right of oversight and the authority to be the final arbiter of the meaning of biblical passages. But exactly how the two parties are to relate to one another is not entirely clear. Historically, there have been tensions between the magisterium and theologians. While church teaching is clear that there cannot be an alternative magisterium, it does not specify how scholars are to exercise their academic freedom within the perspective of faith. Given the sometimes heavy-handed way in which church authorities have acted toward scholars in the past, there is unresolved tension over this point.

The pastoral orientation of the constitution also evinces a certain open-endedness. Although it strongly affirms the positive value that comes from allowing the Scriptures to nourish the soul, nowhere is the process described in detail. In fact, the hermeneutical task (i.e., "interpretation," the process of applying Scripture to modern life) is left quite up in the air, despite the affirmation that Scripture is the "soul of theology" (*DV*, 24). Applying the Bible to modern life in ways that are not reductionist or fundamentalist is not easy, and the text does not spell out how to avoid such pitfalls of biblical interpretation. Indeed, nowhere does the text address the mystery of how the Scriptures are simultaneously old documents and yet perpetually new in the way we understand and apply them. Such tasks are left to professional exegetes and to average laypeople to explore. On the other hand, the constitution's final chapter does call forth a pastoral vision, as Barnabas Ahern enunciated in his analysis of *Dei Verbum*:

> If only the recommendations of this final chapter of the Constitution are followed, a renewal of love for the Scriptures and practical, daily use of the Bible, especially the gospels, will bring fresh and dynamic power into the lives of all the People of God.[13]

One should not, of course, expect that *Dei Verbum* would have addressed all these pertinent issues. When it comes to divine revelation, we are, after all, dealing with a profound mystery. But *Dei Verbum* proved to be a revolutionary document that helped orient the church toward the future in dramatic ways.

PART III
IMPLEMENTATION

Evaluating the implementation of such an important document of the church is inevitably subjective. There are multiple ways to structure this enterprise. I have chosen to delve into five aspects of the implementation of *Dei Verbum*: scholarly assessment, Catholic parish life, priestly formation, official Catholic teaching, and ecumenism. I will then conclude with a few observations about the struggles for the authentic interpretation of the constitution.

SCHOLARLY ASSESSMENT

Vatican II's Dogmatic Constitution on Divine Revelation provoked great interest both within and outside the Catholic Church. The scholarly assessment of *Dei Verbum* was swift and, for the most part, positive. The appearance of *Dei Verbum* caused a flurry of publications, especially in the late 1960s, and then again in the 1980s, surrounding the twentieth and twenty-fifth anniversaries. We will sample some of the scholarly reactions.

The Dutch theologian Edward Schillebeeckx called *Dei Verbum* one of the council's "crown jewels."[1] Noting the "modern and refreshing" character of Vatican II, he pointed to a new spirit in *Dei Verbum*: "For the first time in conciliar history the dynamic development of dogma is given recognition."[2] He also drew attention to the contrast between prior signs of Catholic identity and the one espoused by *Dei Verbum*:

> Whereas altar-and-chalice was formerly, as it were, the symbolism of Catholicism and, obviously, of the counter-Reformation,

59

the bible is now also taken as a symbol of the Catholic Church alongside the chalice. This dogmatic constitution officially spells an end to Catholicism's "counter-Reformation" attitude.[3]

Schillebeeckx's judgment reflected that of many. *Dei Verbum* was seen largely as a turning point in Catholic history. It heralded the success of the truly ecumenical nature of the council called by John XXIII.

Noted American theologian Avery Dulles, an expert in the topic of revelation, echoed this view in his assessment of the council's teaching on revelation in terms of its ecumenical significance.[4] Calling attention to the fact that *Dei Verbum* represented the church's lengthiest and most detailed statement on divine revelation, Dulles affirmed *Dei Verbum*'s assertion of the dynamic nature of revelation and the inseparability of Scripture and Tradition. For Dulles, these details provided evidence that the traditional post-Reformation contrast between Protestantism as a religion of the Word and Catholicism as a religion of the sacraments had come to an end. He especially highlighted the second chapter of the constitution as ecumenically the most important. Specifically drawing attention to article 10, he emphasized, "*Dei Verbum* takes pains to show that the magisterium of the church is not, as some have falsely imagined, the author of tradition."[5] Rather, the church is at the service of the Word. Dulles saw in this change a growth in the church's self-perception that gave it greater impetus for ecumenical ventures.

Even further, Dulles went on to highlight *Dei Verbum*'s dropping of the term "inerrancy" from the final text. For him, this represented the church's embrace of a positive view of Scripture. No longer would the Bible be viewed through a "negative" or restrictive optic in terms of the absence of error. In this fashion, the church showed itself as opposed to the fundamentalist understanding of inspiration in "a rigid and mechanical way."[6] Along with many others, Dulles acknowledged the contribution of Cardinal Bea to the final text of *Dei Verbum*. By calling attention to Bea's credentials as the leading ecumenical proponent of the council, Dulles also asserted that it was no accident he was a biblical scholar.[7] In a sense, the Bible and ecumenism belong together. The extensive sections of *Dei Verbum* on the Bible indeed helped move the ecumenical movement far ahead, as we shall discuss below.

Biblical scholars also weighed in with their assessments of the achievements of *Dei Verbum*. A well-known American scholar, Passionist Father Carroll Stuhlmueller, drew attention to the overlooked contribution of Pope Paul VI in helping to shape *Dei Verbum* by allowing the publication of the PBC's 1964 document, *Sancta Mater Ecclesia*.[8] Chronicling the ebb and flow of the persecution of Catholic biblical scholars since the nineteenth century, Stuhlmueller highlighted especially *Dei Verbum*'s affirmation of the need for scientific study of the sacred writings. In this observation, he would reflect the opinion of most biblical scholars that *Dei Verbum* at least cautiously affirmed this direction for Catholic biblical studies, even if it did not provide a full-blown plan for implementing the scientific investigation of the Bible.

Other biblical scholars drew attention to both the strengths and weaknesses of the dogmatic constitution. Passionist Father Donald Senior, for instance, who was later named to the PBC by Pope John Paul II in 2002, summarized favorably the many contributions of *Dei Verbum* regarding concepts we have already highlighted in Part Two, such as the personalist and dialogical view of revelation, the acknowledgment of the dual human and divine authorship of the Scriptures, the acceptance of both Scripture and Tradition as one source of revelation, the endorsement of historical criticism, and the effective pastoral orientation of the constitution. Nevertheless, he pointed to some significant lacks in the final text, which he attributed primarily to the compromises involved and the battles fought in producing it.[9]

In particular, Senior noted the following weaknesses in *Dei Verbum*:

- the absence of self-criticism with regard to the church's own use of the Scriptures, especially by overlooking the misuse or misinterpretation of the Bible through the centuries
- the unnuanced presentation of apostolic succession and the absence of diverse and pluralistic interpretations that emerge from professional biblical studies
- the rather "grudging" admission of the human dimension of the Scriptures and the lack of deeper acknowledgment of the literary quality of the Bible

- the lack of a more profound ecumenical perspective on the
  Bible, especially with regard to the enduring value of the
  Old Testament and the importance of Judaism in the Cath-
  olic heritage

- the incomplete (if nonetheless positive) pastoral application
  of the Bible for contemporary Catholic life, especially
  regarding the modern challenge of preaching the Word of
  God credibly

If Senior's critique was rather pointed, it did not skimp on admiration for the achievement *Dei Verbum* represented. In the end, he concluded, quite rightly:

> For all its flaws, the *Dogmatic Constitution on Divine Revelation*
> represents an incredible achievement; it is a genuine water-
> shed in the history of Roman Catholicism.[10]

Another American biblical scholar, Jesuit Father Jerome Neyrey,
wrote an essay in a collection on the "unfinished agenda" of Vatican II
on the occasion of the twentieth anniversary of the conclusion of the
council. His essay points to both strengths in *Dei Verbum* and some
unrealized goals. Emphasizing that the constitution was intended primarily as a pastoral guide for the church rather than a treatise for biblical experts, he lauded the following points:

- the emphasis on preaching, both in the sense of the biblical
  roots of the Gospel of Jesus Christ and the contemporary
  pastoral ministry of the ordained (this stance contrasts with
  that of Senior, treated above)

- the concession that revelation, in some sense, develops

- the acknowledgment of the two "authors" of Sacred Scripture, God and the human authors

- the significantly nuanced advance on the understanding of
  how the Gospels came to be, leading to a "qualified endorsement" of the historical-critical method, especially form and
  redaction criticism

– a qualified acceptance of the distinction between the Jesus of history, as portrayed in the Gospels, and the Christ of faith, as proclaimed in the Gospels and in the life of the church

For all the strengths of *Dei Verbum*, Neyrey did not let pass the importance of the PBC document *Sancta Mater Ecclesia* in shaping the final text. As we saw in Part One, this text, indeed, made a strong imprint on the constitution. The PBC in some ways helped to reorient the final text in a forward-looking direction, based upon the results of sound biblical scholarship at the time. Yet in setting forth a future agenda beyond the constitution, Neyrey noted several deficiencies (not actually "criticisms"), some of which were tied to the strengths he had listed. According to Neyrey, there was insufficient acknowledgment of the distinctions of each of the four Gospels in their portrayal of the life of Jesus, and no hint that the evangelists might actually have composed parts of the Gospels. Also, in general, Neyrey saw the need for further work on the relationship between "history" and "truth" in the Bible, something not entirely solved by *Dei Verbum*'s approach to inspiration and inerrancy.

One prominent Jesuit biblical scholar, John R. Donahue, has written extensively on the Catholic approach to the Bible since Vatican II.[12] Many of his articles have involved summaries of *Dei Verbum* and the agenda that has emerged from it. He has particularly noted the dual message of the constitution in both encouraging historical-critical study of the Bible and in issuing cautions about the importance of traditional theological and spiritual interpretations of Scripture. His assessment largely reflects many of the comments above, but he has also pointed out the contribution that the post–Vatican II approach to Scripture has made in the area of social justice.[13] While other documents from Vatican II (e.g., *GS*) could be said to be more explicitly concerned with justice and peace issues, Donahue points out how far the new approach to the Bible promoted by *Dei Verbum* influenced the shape of many of the church's subsequent teachings. He thus provides evidence for the far-reaching consequences of *Dei Verbum* in the decades after the council.

Protestant scholars also weighed in concerning their assessment of *Dei Verbum*. During the debates over the schemas, some of the

Protestant observers at the council were amazed at the openness and frankness of the discussions. One well-known Lutheran observer, George Quandbeck, commented on the incredible diversity of opinions among the council fathers when it came to difficult questions like the relationship of Tradition and Scripture or how to speak of inspiration and inerrancy.[14]

During one post-conciliar conference held at the University of Notre Dame in 1966 to discuss and analyze the significance of the council, Paul S. Minear, a prominent Protestant biblical scholar, affirmed *Dei Verbum* for its dialogical treatment of Scripture as a living document. But he also pronounced himself "quite baffled" by the constitution's bewildering treatment of the notion of Tradition, which he found too fluid and unfocused.[15] In particular, he thought that the concept seemed to make no particular distinction between the transmission of the Tradition and its content. In fact, his critique points out a limitation of *Dei Verbum* that most scholars would quickly acknowledge, namely, the lack of clarity in the concept of Tradition and how to explain the exact relationship between Scripture and Tradition.

These comments offer a representative sampling of scholarly reactions to *Dei Verbum*. By and large, the implementation of the document from a scholarly angle would, even forty years later, be viewed quite positively, both from Catholic and non-Catholic vantage points.

CATHOLIC PARISH LIFE

Dei Verbum was one of the last documents of Vatican II to be approved, but its impact was almost immediate, even on the pastoral level. Catholics were "ripe" for a rediscovery of the Bible. Some four hundred years had passed since the Protestant Reformation, and Catholics had defined themselves vis-à-vis Protestants, who emphasized the Word of God, primarily as a people of "the sacraments." They hungered to know more about the Bible.

Not that Catholics then abandoned the sacraments. On the contrary, liturgical reform and biblical rebirth went hand in hand. Both the liturgical movement and the biblical movement were, as we pointed out in Part One, well under way when Vatican II convened.

Sacramental reform was almost immediate in the church after the council, especially with regard to the Eucharist. One Sunday the Mass was in Latin and the priest had his back to the people; the next Sunday it was in English and the priest was facing the people. But the reform was even broader, for one of the great effects of the council was to insist that the celebration of every sacrament be accompanied by a reading from Scripture, even if it were merely a sentence or two.

The liturgical reforms, however, touched the Bible directly in another way. The readings of the liturgical year were expanded and reorganized into a three-year lectionary cycle, to be read in the vernacular rather than in Latin. Each year is now devoted to one of the Synoptic Gospels (Matthew for Year A, Mark for Year B, Luke for Year C), with John used annually throughout the seasons of Lent and Easter or to supplement Year B. On each Sunday the readings usually consist of an Old Testament reading, followed by a psalm response, a reading from a New Testament letter, and a gospel reading. (The Easter season is an exception; the first reading is from the Acts of the Apostles, because it tells the story of the early church.) Catholics began to hear proclaimed at Sunday Mass (and at weekday Masses, on a two-year cycle) large, sequential sections of the Bible, passages that they had previously never heard at Mass. Inevitably, this development sparked interest in knowing more about the Bible. Developments took off in two directions: academic and formal studies on the one hand, and Bible studies for laity on the other.

Now backed by a dogmatic constitution,[16] Catholic biblical scholars, who had quietly been doing their research all along since even before the time of *Divino Afflante Spiritu*, began to publish more. Several Catholic publishing houses sprang up almost overnight, and those already in existence turned their attention to disseminating the council's teaching, especially in the area of biblical studies. They created commentary series, designed study Bibles and Bible dictionaries, and produced catechetical resources that tried to capitalize on *Dei Verbum*'s emphasis on the Word of God.

In the 1960s in the United States, three names in particular emerged in Catholic biblical studies: Raymond E. Brown, SS, Joseph A. Fitzmyer, SJ, and Roland E. Murphy, O.Carm. These three giants took on the enormous task of publishing the first all-Catholic one-volume commentary on the Bible that utilized modern scientific methods of inquiry, *The Jerome Biblical Commentary* (1968). Produced only three years after *Dei Verbum*, it quickly became a best seller. In a sense, this publication, more than any other, marked Catholic biblical scholarship come of age, the first fruits of the council's earnest desire to promote the Word of God. The same three editors produced a totally revised and updated version in 1990, *The New Jerome Biblical Commentary*, which has also become a staple resource for biblical interpretation. Both volumes contain a wealth of material on the history and exercise of the Catholic approach to the Bible.

After the council, Catholic scholars began to exert more influence in biblical studies. They quickly advanced in expertise to be able to participate in technical discussions with their Protestant and Jewish counterparts. They joined more fully in the life of the "academy," that is, in engaging their non-Catholic colleagues freely in scholarly discourse. They also collaborated on the production of new ecumenical Bible translations, such as the New English Bible (1970), the Revised Standard Version (2nd ed., 1971), and the New Revised Standard Version (1989), and invited Protestant scholars to join in the production of Catholic translations (e.g., The New American Bible, 1970).

Ultimately, Catholic participation in biblical studies flourished. Indeed, the Society of Biblical Literature, one of the most prestigious societies for biblical scholars, elected John L. McKenzie its first Catholic president quite rapidly after the council, in 1966. He was to be followed by several others, including Raymond E. Brown (1977), Joseph A. Fitzmyer (1979), Roland E. Murphy (1984), Elisabeth Schüssler Fiorenza (1987), Harold W. Attridge (2001), John J. Collins (2002), and, most recently, Carolyn Osiek (2005). While *Dei Verbum* did not cause this to happen, it was the driving force behind promoting Catholic biblical scholars to exercise their expertise freely at the service of both the church and the academy.

Dei Verbum impacted Catholic life on a popular level as well. By the late 1960s many Catholic parishes had instituted Bible education programs for children and for adults. Catholic publishers began to produce long-term Bible study programs (e.g., Little Rock Scripture Study and the Denver Program, to name two), based on sound scholarship, that could be used for adult instruction. More and more textbooks for catechetical instruction included greater tracts on the Bible and emphasized learning basic Bible stories. In addition, for a time, many parishes adopted a "lectionary-based" approach to catechetics that was intended to utilize the lectionary as a basis for Catholic instruction.

Some critics of these catechetical developments point out limitations in their materials, at least from the perspective of biblical scholars or theologians. At times, for instance, few advances in the scientific knowledge of Scripture seem to have made their way into some of these textbooks, which continue to espouse naïve views of the interpretation of particular passages. Furthermore, from a theological perspective, making the lectionary the sole basis of catechetical instruction can limit the ability to impart to students the broader content of the Catholic faith. Such mixed reviews, however, do not detract from the fact that post–Vatican II catechetical instruction now includes biblical components in one form or another.

On the popular level, magazines like *The Bible Today* fostered good instruction on a basic level for laity interested in learning more about the Bible. Passionist Father Barnabas Ahern (d. 1995), in fact, who was a decisive influence at the council with regard to *Dei Verbum*, had been the first editor of *The Bible Today*, which began publication in 1962, the year the council convened. The expressed purpose of this popular journal was to foster Bible study in light of the insights of the scientific method.[17] On a more technical level was *Biblical Theology Bulletin*, which quickly turned its attention to newer scientific methods of biblical studies, such as social scientific criticism. From a different angle altogether was the appeal of biblical archaeology magazines (e.g., *Biblical Archaeology Review* and *Biblical Archaeology*) or television programs (e.g., *Mysteries of the Bible*) that attempt to disseminate information about recent archaeological finds, in the Holy Land or elsewhere, that affect our knowledge of biblical history. At times marketing interests seem to outweigh prudence in the way some topics are treated, and sensationalist claims abound. But such resources confirm an intense interest in the Bible that, at least for Catholics, evolved from Vatican II.

Individually, of course, on the eve of the council or in its immediate wake, many Catholic biblical scholars published popular works (books, tapes, videos) in addition to their scholarly tomes. John L. McKenzie's book, *The Two-Edged Sword* (1956), was a classic introduction to the Old Testament on a popular level. Later, his masterful *Dictionary of the Bible* (1965) also put into lay hands an invaluable resource that disseminated the results of modern biblical scholarship. The Liturgical Press also published a series of smaller works called the *Old Testament Reading Guide* and *New Testament Reading Guide* (1960–1965), edited by Ahern and Mother Kathryn Sullivan, RSCJ, an early pioneer in American biblical studies. Later, the Liturgical Press produced short, popular commentaries on each book of the Bible in the form of small booklets that would eventually be revised, updated, and collected together into in a one-volume format, *The Collegeville Bible Commentary* (1989). An entirely new, revised set of these commentary booklets began to appear in 2005, written generally by a new group of biblical scholars. Michael Glazier, too, produced popular commentaries on books from both Testaments (Old Testament Message and New Testament Message) that demonstrated the expertise of Catholic scholars and the broad appeal that commentaries could have among the general public.

More recently, Catholic publishers continue to produce useful commentaries on the Bible. For example, on a popular level New City Press (of the Focolare Movement) has published short, readable commentaries that emphasize the spiritual message of the books of the Bible ("Spiritual Commentaries"). For more advanced readers, such as seminarians, pastors, and professionals, the Liturgical Press has published two excellent commentary series that show the tremendous advances in Catholic scholarship since the end of the council. Reviewers have lauded these series, *Berit Olam* (Old Testament) and *Sacra Pagina* (New Testament), as fine examples of scientifically oriented interpretation sensitively applied to the deeper and spiritual message of the biblical books. My point here is that the influence on scholars begun by *Dei Verbum* continues into the present, for the benefit of both the church and the academy.

One could also list the multiple publications on a popular level of the great Sulpician-Jesuit-Carmelite triumvirate whom we have mentioned before, Raymond E. Brown, Roland E. Murphy, and Joseph. A. Fitzmyer, among many others. Just to name a few of the more well-known scholars (alphabetically): Dianne Bergant, CSA, Lawrence Boadt, CSP, Brendan Byrne, SJ, Richard Clifford, SJ, John R. Donahue, SJ, Daniel J. Harrington, SJ, Frank J. Matera, John P. Meier, Francis

Moloney, SDB, Jerome Murphy-O'Connor, Carolyn Osiek, RSCJ, Pheme Perkins, Sandra Schneiders, IHM, and Donald Senior, CP. It should be emphasized that these scholars had predecessors who were just as great but whose names would be much less well known because the times did not encourage popularization of scientific biblical studies. Such scholars included Edward Arbez, SS, Francis Gigot, SS, and Edward Siegman, CPPS. The work of all these dedicated scholars and their colleagues is testimony to the sincere efforts to take *Dei Verbum* to heart to foster familiarity with the Bible as broadly as possible (*DV*, 22 and 24).

PRIESTLY FORMATION

A third way in which *Dei Verbum* impacted Catholic life was in the training of priests. The constitution explicitly said that

> all the clergy must hold fast to the Sacred Scriptures through diligent sacred reading and careful study, especially the priests of Christ and others, such as deacons and catechists who are legitimately active in the ministry of the word. This is to be done so that none of them will become "an empty preacher of the word of God outwardly, who is not a listener to it inwardly." (*DV*, 25)

This was clearly a call to make the Word of God more central in the education of the church's key pastoral leaders (as expressed also in *PO*, 4). This meant a reexamination of seminary instruction.

If one were to ask priests ordained prior to Vatican II about their instruction in biblical studies, they would usually bemoan the fact that it was woefully lacking. Unless they were fortunate enough to have had an exceptional professor who happened to be advanced in his knowledge of the historical-critical method, as some were, training in the Bible took a back seat to other instruction. Whereas previous seminary training had emphasized moral theology, canon law, and the "manual" tradition of theology, instruction in biblical studies in Roman Catholic seminaries after the council became more central and more demanding. This was due, in part, to the advanced education that many Catholic scholars were now receiving, not only in Roman universities but also in secular and Protestant schools around the globe. It was also a response to *Dei Verbum*'s clarion call to have the Bible influence Catholic life more concretely (*DV*, 24 and 25).

This advance in the seminary curriculum coincided with an emphasis on homiletic instruction that was biblically based. Prior to Vatican II, priests generally were taught to deliver Sunday "sermons," which usually had no relation to the Scripture readings of the day. Rather, preachers tended to orient their sermons toward moral instruction or explanations of church teachings, doctrines, or spiritual themes, or the example of Christian piety seen in the Virgin Mary and the saints. After Vatican II, however, there was a significant shift. Priests were expected to deliver "homilies" that were supposed to help explain the Scriptures within the context of the church's faith (*SC*, 51 and 52). *Dei Verbum* also emphasized that the Scriptures should nourish preaching (*DV*, 21). Consequently, it was essential to provide proper training in both homiletics and in knowledge of the Bible in order to meet this goal. In reality, seminarians generally thirsted for more biblical studies both out of personal interest and to provide them with a firm foundation for the task of preaching. In some instances, seminaries have even experimented with team teaching by biblical and homiletics professors.

While some would suggest that contemporary Roman Catholic preaching still is not as inspiring as it should be, seminary instruction—specifically in biblical studies—nevertheless greatly improved after the council. If there is still a need for more effective implementation of the ideal put forth at the council, it is not for want of a worthy pastoral goal expressed in *Dei Verbum*. In fact, Pope John Paul II's outstanding apostolic exhortation on priests, *Pastores Dabo Vobis*, highlights the importance of Scripture in priestly formation precisely because being a minister of the Word is one of the three most important ministries of priests (the other two being the sacraments and pastoral charity). The pope writes: "For this reason, the priest himself ought first of all to develop a great personal familiarity with the word of God" (*PDV*, 26 and 54). Good training in both biblical studies and homiletics remains a prominent feature of post-Vatican II seminary formation.

OFFICIAL CATHOLIC TEACHING

Another way in which *Dei Verbum* exercised a broad influence in the life of the church has been through the use of Scripture in official documents. This is true of papal pronouncements, such as encyclical letters, and of documents issued by various episcopal conferences. Some examples will suffice.

During the late Pope John Paul II's lengthy pontificate (1978–2005), many of his encyclical letters and apostolic exhortations used Scripture as their basic inspiration. Shortly after his election as pope, for example, he devoted 129 Wednesday audiences to an exposition of a "theology of the body" based upon the early chapters of Genesis, the letters of Saint Paul, and the four Gospels. Eventually published together in one volume, some of these early talks utilized modern (if somewhat dated) critical methods with regard to the Old Testament texts.[18]

Even more examples are found in his later writings, especially his encyclical letters. *Mane Nobiscum Domine* ("Remain with Us, Lord"—on the Eucharist, published in 2004) makes prominent use of Luke 24 (among other texts, such as Matthew 28:20 and John 15:4). *Pastores Dabo Vobis* ("I Will Give You Shepherds"—published in 1992 as a result of the 1990 synod on priestly formation) takes as its inspiration a text from Jeremiah 3:15, but also uses many other biblical texts to support the basic elements of priestly formation in our day. Two important encyclicals on morality, truth, and the sacredness of human life also draw on biblical texts for inspiration and basic orientation, e.g., *Veritatis Splendor* ("The Splendor of Truth"—1993), which uses the story of the rich young man (Matt 19:16–25), and *Evangelium Vitae* ("The Gospel of Life"—1995), which uses many Old and New Testament texts on the sanctity of human life. Finally, the pope again used the early chapters of Genesis (chapters 1–3) for an encyclical on the dignity of human work, *Laborem Exercens* ("On Human Work"—1981) and for a lengthy treatment of social justice issues, *Sollicitudo Rei Socialis* ("On Social Concerns"—1987).

An analysis of this pope's use of Scripture, however, shows that, for the most part, he preferred spiritual interpretations and applications of the Bible to historical and scientific interpretations.[19] He rarely employed the historical-critical method and was clearly more at home in pre-critical approaches. Some might see in this a backtracking, but I do not think it necessary to see such "spiritualizing" of Scripture as totally opposed to modern interpretive methods, something we will discuss in Part Four. What I think is more important is the pope's insistence that the Bible continues to have relevance today. John Paul II (Karol Wojtyla, then the young archbishop of Krakow) was himself a participant at Vatican II, though his contributions were in other areas and not so much to *Dei Verbum*. (In 1968, however, he did write a short commentary in Polish on the constitution.) In his personal application of the Bible to his Petrine ministry, he took to heart *Dei Verbum*'s encouragement of Catholics to make regular use of Scripture for their spiritual well-being. In this regard, part of John Paul II's legacy will likely be the deference he showed to Scripture in fulfillment of *Dei Verbum*'s pastoral goal of nourishing the faithful.

If I may add one other example from the pontificate of John Paul II, it is the promulgation of the "luminous mysteries" of the rosary (also called "the mysteries of light"). For some, the rosary represents a pious devotion that has little to do with the Bible. It began in the Middles Ages as a popular substitute for the liturgy of the hours, which was primarily the prayer of the ordained (*CCC*, 2678). In reality, the rosary is a prayer form that does relate to the Bible, for the mysteries one meditates upon during its recitation are taken from the life of Christ. In 2002 John Paul II published his apostolic letter, *Rosarium Virginis Mariae* ("The Rosary of the Virgin Mary"). In it he proposed adding another set of "mysteries" to the rosary (in addition to the traditional sorrowful, joyful, and glorious mysteries) in which further events from the life of Christ recounted in the Gospels would be the focus. These are: the baptism of Jesus, the wedding at Cana, the proclamation of the kingdom of God, the transfiguration, and the first Eucharist [Last Supper]. By doing this, he emphasized the importance of reflecting on the biblical stories of the life of Christ for personal enrichment, and thus contributed to the broader use of the Bible in Catholic piety.

Popes are not the only ones to have utilized the Bible in their teachings. After Vatican II, there was a new sense of the importance of episcopal conferences as a way for bishops in a geographic region to cooperate in fostering the faith in their region and guiding their people.

These conferences frequently issue pastoral letters or other weighty teachings. Two important examples come from the conference of bishops in the United States (now called the United States Conference of Catholic Bishops [USCCB])— "The Challenge of Peace" (1983) and "Economic Justice for All" (1985). These two documents contain lengthy sections expounding the biblical background to the timely topics of world peace and economic justice. Many pastoral letters, either of episcopal conferences or individual bishops, have subsequently followed this pattern. They incorporate some aspect of Scripture either as a lead-in to the topic at hand or as support throughout the document.

At times, of course, some of this biblical application can lean toward a problematic type of "proof texting." Passages from the Bible sometimes are taken out of context and made to fit into a preconceived framework, thus assuming a meaning not inherent in the text. This is a constant danger in such endeavors. But often the tone of such documents transcends this approach. At the very least, the Scriptures are seen as laying essential foundations for later church teaching or perhaps offering an inspiring and poetic vision of the modern mission of the church. In this regard, the Scriptures now inform the contemporary life and teaching of the Catholic Church in ways far beyond what was imagined prior to Vatican II.

Dei Verbum also made an impact on the production of the *Catechism of the Catholic Church* (first ed., 1994, 2nd ed., 1997). For many years after the council, some Catholics lamented the lack of a succinct but thorough source book of Catholic doctrine. They wanted a convenient compendium of the basic teachings of the Catholic faith, one that could be easily consulted for answers to common questions. Many American Catholics, especially, had been reared in the era of *The Baltimore Catechism*, the well-known question-and-answer compendium of Catholic doctrine that made it easy to memorize these teachings. They missed that functional approach. So in 1986 Pope John Paul II formed a commission to design a new catechism that would fill this gap. He promulgated the Catechism in 1992 in his apostolic constitution, *Fidei Depositum* ("The Deposit of Faith"). The Catechism cites *Dei Verbum* some seventy-seven times, making it the fourth most cited council document in the text (after *Gaudium et Spes*, *Lumen Gentium*, and *Sacrosanctum Concilium*, in descending order).

Understandably, the Catechism uses *Dei Verbum* frequently in chapter 2, "God Comes to Meet Man," which deals with revelation and Sacred Scripture (*CCC*, 51–141).[20] The section on the transmission of divine revelation (*CCC*, 74–100) makes extensive use of *Dei Verbum*, emphasizing the apostolic tradition, the unity of Scripture and Tradition, and the role of the magisterium in preserving and fostering the faith.

Moreover, the very outline of the section on Scripture (*CCC*, 101–33) imitates *Dei Verbum* in its christological orientation and explanation of Scripture. It begins with an exposition of Christ as the incarnate Word of God (*CCC*, 101–4). Then it proceeds to the question of inspiration and the truth to be found in the sacred writings (*CCC*, 105–8). It contains a section on the Holy Spirit as the main interpreter of Scripture (*CCC*, 109–19), including a discussion of the traditional "senses" of Scripture from the Middle Ages (namely, the literal, allegorical, moral, and anagogical senses of Scripture, not specifically discussed in *Dei Verbum*). The next section lays out the church's understanding of the canon of Sacred Scripture, with distinct expositions of the Old Testament, the New Testament, and the unity of both Testaments (*CCC*, 120–30). Finally, it concludes with a practical section on the role of Scripture in the life of the church (*CCC*, 131–33). Even though the Catechism uses other resources as the basis for its discussion, this general outline flows precisely from that of *Dei Verbum*.

Dei Verbum exercised a further important influence on the Catechism. The Catechism sets forth a Catholic approach to Scripture in direct accord with three principles from the dogmatic constitution:

1. Attend to the "content and unity" of all Sacred Scripture.

2. Read the Bible in the context of the church's "living Tradition."

3. Keep in mind the unified nature of revelation, i.e., the "coherence" of all the truths God has revealed in the faith. (*CCC*, 112–14; see *DV*, 12)

Chapter 2 of the Catechism is like a thumbnail sketch of a Catholic approach to Scripture. Like *Dei Verbum*, it places biblical interpretation within the living Tradition of the church. It assumes the complex interrelationship between Scripture and Tradition that is at the heart of the Catholic faith. It also emphasizes that there is a coherent unity in Scripture that must be honored. One cannot simply interpret one passage or another from the Bible apart from the testimony of the whole canon of Sacred Scripture. Such an approach, which *Dei Verbum* outlines, militates against taking passages out of context and consequently misinterpreting them. It also further distances a Catholic approach from that of biblical fundamentalists.

Just as important is the Catechism's adoption of *Dei Verbum*'s outline of the levels of historical tradition contained in the canonical Gospels (*CCC*, 126; see *DV*, 19), which, as we saw in Part Two, came from the PBC's document, *Sancta Mater Ecclesia*. This approach enshrines in the Catholic exposition of Scripture the understanding that the Gospels contain layered traditions rooted in the oral, written, and edited sources of the evangelists. Exegetes must carefully sift through these layers to explore the multiple aspects of meaning contained therein. By drawing attention to this process, the Catechism implements one aspect of the constitution that has become standard in biblical scholarship. In short, the Catechism uses *Dei Verbum* extensively as a solid platform for its summary of the Catholic faith.

Before moving to the next topic, a few additional observations are necessary to round out our discussion of the Catechism. I mentioned above the Catechism's discussion of the four "senses" of Scripture that come from ancient patristic and medieval tradition (*CCC*, 115–19). These are the literal, the allegorical, the moral, and the anagogical senses of Scripture, which deserve greater explanation.

Dei Verbum does not deal with the literal sense of Scripture directly. It does, however, seem to equate it with the "meaning the sacred authors really intended" (*DV*, 12). The Catechism affirms the literal sense of Scripture as foundational to the other senses. The literal meaning provides the proper platform for moving to other levels of meaning in the text. But the Catechism rightly does not *restrict* interpretation only to the literal sense.

Using the overarching category of the "spiritual senses" of Scripture, the Catechism mentions the three deeper senses that patristic and medieval interpreters espoused, i.e., the allegorical, the moral, and the anagogical. The allegorical sense deals with correspondences within the Scriptures, especially those between the Old and New Testaments. One allegorical method is typological interpretation, in which a figure from the Old Testament is seen as "type" or model of a figure in the New Testament (e.g., Adam as a "type" of Christ [Rom 5:14]). The moral sense, of course, expresses the strong ethical character of the Scripture and is particularly useful for instruction in ethical matters. The anagogical sense pertains to the profound meaning of Scripture that leads to our salvation in the kingdom of God. It expresses the salvific dimensions of Scripture that deepen our faith. After summarizing these senses, which are not explicitly referenced in *Dei Verbum*, the Catechism quotes the passage from the constitution that affirms the church's ultimate right and duty to announce the definitive interpretation of the Bible (*DV*, 12). Thus, the church is obliged to watch over carefully and direct the process of interpretation to ensure that the authentic meaning of the Scriptures is encountered.

These points are important for an understanding of Catholic teaching on Scripture. Although *Dei Verbum* does not treat them explicitly, it does emphasize that the Bible contains the truth necessary for salvation (*DV*, 11). Its message therefore is never restricted only to the literal sense. Openness to deeper meanings within Scripture is a hallmark of the Catholic approach, and the Catechism adopts traditional categories to expound it.

Some scholars, we should note, have detected certain limitations in the Catechism's *applications* of Scripture. At times, the Catechism does not acknowledge tensions within the Bible. One example is the treatment of the covenant with the Jews. Highlighting the importance of the Old Testament for Christianity, the Catechism rightly affirms that it remains permanently valid (*CCC*, 121). Yet this position is stated so simplistically that it overlooks the fact that the New Testament itself expresses mixed views about this issue (cf. Rom 11:29 and Heb 8:13), resulting in a certain tension within the biblical text that cannot be ignored.

Others have criticized the tendency in the Catechism still to employ proof texts. They maintain that it exhibits a kind of stilted use of Scripture more characteristic of an earlier era. One example is the lack of sophistication regarding the historical basis of the Gospels in the section on the life of Christ (*CCC*, 484–658). The results of the historical-critical method in this regard seem to have slipped into the background, as if they were totally insignificant.

Yet another criticism is the extremely limited use of Scripture throughout the Catechism to bolster doctrinal and moral teachings, in comparison to the extensive use of magisterial documents. Some view this as a lessening of the importance of the Bible for Catholic teaching, although I doubt that the framers of the Catechism intended this. Also, some would draw attention to the fact that, despite *Dei Verbum*'s promotion of the Bible for spiritual enrichment (*DV*, 21 and 25), the Catechism does not give explicit guidance (beyond affirming *lectio divina*, the ancient practice of meditation on Bible passages) on *how* to accomplish this in a way that allows for modern application and spiritual inspiration without distortion of the text.

Despite these limitations, the Catechism incorporates *Dei Verbum* into its presentation of the theme of divine revelation in a manner that confirms the constitution's lasting value for Catholic faith.

ECUMENISM

Further testimony to the broad influence of *Dei Verbum* can be found in the significant ecumenical projects that flourished in the wake of Vatican II.

One such project was the establishment in 1969 of an ecumenically oriented organization to promote Bible study worldwide. This was part of Cardinal Bea's vision in 1967, after the conclusion of the council, when he invited existing Catholic biblical organizations to join in promoting good Bible study. Only in 1969 did a new organ to promote the Bible come into existence. Cardinal Johannes Willebrands, Bea's successor as the head of the Secretariat for Promoting Christian Unity, established the Catholic Biblical Federation (CBF) in direct response to the constitution's call to make Sacred Scripture more accessible to all Christians (*DV*, 22).

Now the federation promotes biblical studies around the world, and it sponsors periodic conferences to discuss related topics. In fact, for the fortieth anniversary of *Dei Verbum*, the federation co-sponsored with the Pontifical Council for Promoting Christian Unity an international congress in Rome (September 14–18, 2005), at which biblical experts and church authorities from around the world spoke. Unlike the PBC, which works directly under the Congregation for the Doctrine of the Faith, the CBF is more pastoral than academic in its orientation. It designs programs, supports Bible translation projects, promotes Bible study in small Christian communities worldwide, and publishes a newsletter (*Bulletin* Dei Verbum). The late Pope John Paul II encouraged the work of the federation following the bishops' synod of 1985, at which many bishops noted that *Dei Verbum* had been neglected and deserved greater attention.[21] He called on the CBF to help implement the constitution's vision and to find new and creative ways to promote the Bible.

An even more significant ecumenical step occurred with the initiation of formal dialogues between the Roman Catholic Church and various other denominations, such as Lutherans, Anglicans, Baptists, Methodists, Evangelicals, Orthodox, and Pentecostals. Some of these dialogues have been more extensive than others. Two, in particular, have produced profound studies of important theological and ecclesial issues that, in turn, have helped promote ecumenism: the Lutheran-Catholic and Anglican-Catholic dialogues.

The Lutheran-Catholic dialogue has been particularly productive. It has resulted in numerous studies that have advanced understanding and cooperation between the two churches. Biblical studies, in particular, have been at the forefront of these ecumenical discussions. Three are especially worth mentioning.

Peter in the New Testament (1973),[22] edited by one Catholic and two Lutheran biblical scholars (Raymond E. Brown, Karl P. Donfried, and John Reumann), explores the biblical data on the image of Peter (and the "Petrine office," as it were) as it developed throughout the New Testament. The findings explicitly were intended to help the two denominations reflect seriously on the nature of the papacy and its roots in the New Testament.

A second study tackled another delicate topic, the role of Mary, the mother of Jesus. The same three editors, joined by another Roman Catholic (Joseph A. Fitzmyer), produced a volume of essays titled, *Mary in the New Testament* (1978).[23] This book offers an in-depth evaluation of the biblical data on Mary, with a view to promoting better understanding of each denomination's perspective on Mary's role in salvation history.

A third volume tackled the thorny topic of justification by faith, a key element of the Lutheran faith. Titled *Righteousness in the New Testament* (1982), this volume was prepared by Lutheran John Reumann, with responses by Catholics Joseph A. Fitzmyer and Jerome A. Quinn.[24] The book was instrumental in overcoming caricatures of each denomination's positions regarding salvation and the interpretation of the Pauline letters.

While such studies may seem unimportant in and of themselves, they have borne great fruit. In the case of the Roman Catholic-Lutheran dialogues, one significant advance in mutual understanding occurred on the eve of the third Christian millennium. I refer to the remarkable accord celebrated on Reformation Day, October 31, 1999, in Augsburg, Germany. Officials of the Roman Catholic Church and the Lutheran World Federation signed two documents outlining the basic areas of *agreement* on the biblical notion of justification by faith: *Joint Declaration on the Doctrine of Justification* and *Official Common Statement* (with an *Annex*).

This remarkable development would never have occurred without the groundwork laid by biblical scholars, both Catholic and Lutheran. Although not every single detail in the doctrine of justification has been addressed satisfactorily yet (as noted in the *Annex*), the agreement is nonetheless historic. It proclaims that, despite the tragic history of the Reformation and Counter-Reformation, Catholics and Lutherans do have essentially a common understanding of God's salvation of humanity. This judgment indeed fits neatly with *Dei Verbum*, which proclaims that the very purpose of divine revelation is the salvation of all people (*DV*, 2).

A second set of dialogues has been particularly fruitful as well, namely, that between Anglicans and Roman Catholics. In 1966 Pope Paul VI and Michael Ramsey, then archbishop of Canterbury, established a commission to explore the question of possible unity of the two denominations. It was called the Anglican-Roman Catholic International Commission (ARCIC). A group of bishops and scholars representing each church gathered on a regular basis until 1981, tackling many issues such as the Eucharist, ordained ministry in the church, and the papacy and the exercise of authority. A final report was issued in 1982. Formal responses by the leaders of both denominations were quite positive, but Roman Catholic leaders remained concerned with the questions of Eucharist and the ordained ministry. The result has been the continuation of ongoing dialogues into the present, especially here in the United States.

In addition to the two successful dialogues mentioned above, I wish to draw attention to an even more dramatic, if much less extensive, development, namely, the dialogue between the Roman Catholic Church and the Southern Baptist Convention. In 1999 representatives from both churches issued a brief statement outlining serious differences of approach to the Bible but also emphasizing how much each side had learned from the other.[25] They specifically included a review of *Dei Verbum* in their study, as well as exegesis of selected biblical texts. Southern Baptists belong to the more fundamentalist wing of Evangelical Christianity, so differences were to be expected. Remarkably, this short statement outlines succinctly and forthrightly diverse approaches to inerrancy and biblical interpretation. In the end, the two groups of participants agreed to disagree, but they also pledged to continue exploring these and related issues in the future. This development could scarcely have been imagined without the influence of *Dei Verbum*.

Formal dialogues between Christian churches are one form of ecumenical advance, but there are also others on a more local level. For example, many instances of cooperation between Protestants and Catholics occurred on the level of theological education after Vatican II. Various seminaries, theological schools, and parishes sponsored (and still do sponsor) ecumenical events, especially during the week of prayer for Christian unity (January 18–25) that culminates in the feast of one of the most important human authors of the Bible, Saint Paul. In 1968, St. Mary's Seminary and University in Baltimore, the oldest Catholic seminary in the United States (1791), founded an Ecumenical Institute (quickly dubbed the "EI") that has flourished to this day. In fact, under the leadership of the present dean, Michael Gorman, the institute published in 2005 a unique ecumenical introduction to the Bible, written by faculty members representing many different denominations.[26] Cooperative ventures like these not only have promoted good biblical studies but also have fostered an open spirit of dialogue that continues to work toward that elusive, deeper Christian unity so sought by Pope John XXIII and his successors.

Dei Verbum must be credited with giving the proper boost to such promising developments. Biblical scholarship alone cannot resolve the many different theological and ecclesial issues that confront ecumenical dialogues and ventures. Systematic theologians, among others, must participate (and have participated) in further steps in these dialogues. In fact, theologians like Edward Schillebeeckx and Walter Kasper used insights from modern biblical scholarship to produce important studies in Christology after the council.[27] The Bible is absolutely foundational for these initiatives. Without some understanding of both methodology and interpretation of critical biblical passages, these ecumenical projects would go nowhere. As it is, the direction set in motion by *Dei Verbum* has led to significant ecumenical developments.

This short survey is not meant to imply that *Dei Verbum* single-handedly accomplished a revolution. The implementation of this dogmatic constitution was simultaneously swift and incremental. Some of these developments had been in the making for years before the council. We must remember also that other documents from the council had great influence, especially in the area of ecumenism. Yet one must not forget that the Bible is one area where Christians can find (and have found) a lot of common ground, despite theological differences and specific questions of interpretation that can vary.

STRUGGLES FOR AUTHENTIC INTERPRETATION

There is at least one note of caution that must be sounded in this otherwise laudatory exposition of the impact of *Dei Verbum*. The direction of the Roman Catholic Church in the post–Vatican II era has not pleased everyone. Ideological divisions among Catholics have become quite apparent. *Dei Verbum* is one of the council's more controversial documents that, perhaps due to its historical roots in the debates at the council, has fostered a tug of war between so-called conservatives and liberals within the church. At issue is authentic interpretation of the constitution itself. The lightning rod for this division has generally been the application of the historical-critical method. I say this for three reasons.

First, not everyone believes that the constitution's acceptance of the historical-critical method of the Bible is proper. Some critics have judged that the Catholic approach to the Bible has become too "Protestant," and they directly attribute this to the predominance of the historical-critical method. (The method did, after all, emerge in the nineteenth century from largely German Protestant universities.) Some even attempt to argue, unpersuasively in my judgment, that to interpret *Dei Verbum* as fostering the historical-critical method is a misreading of the constitution. There is, in fact, a revisionist movement under way to rethink the ramifications of Vatican II, with specific attention to *Dei Verbum*.

While some of this is necessary and understandable on the occasion of a major anniversary, to some degree it reflects dissatisfaction with the final outcome of the council. For some Catholics, things have gone too far. They want to see a pullback from some modern advances, and thus there is the desire to reinterpret what *Dei Verbum* really taught. As I attempted to show in Part Two, the constitution clearly did enshrine the historical-critical method. However, nowhere did *Dei Verbum* make it the exclusive method for biblical study. There is much room for a variety of methods of biblical study, from the ancient patristic to the postmodern approaches, but we will return to this issue in Part Four.

Second, there is also a question of whether the historical-critical method should itself be applied to church teachings, such as the documents of Vatican II. Raymond E. Brown, who is justly seen as one of the greatest Catholic biblical scholars of the twentieth century, devoted many of his popular lectures to addressing this issue.[28] Through popular articles and books, he attempted to show just how much at the service of the church this scientific method can be. He also maintained, with the support of many other Catholic scholars, that this same method could and must be applied to church teachings themselves. Context is vitally important to understanding. Only if church documents are, like the Scriptures, placed in their historical context can we understand them properly. That is why, in Part One of this book, I tried to give some attention to the historical setting of the council and the precedents in church teaching that were in place before it convened. This is also why we are fortunate to live in a time when excellent historical studies and memoirs are being published on the history of Vatican II. As we look toward the fiftieth anniversary of the council, we can hope that our evaluative abilities will have sharpened even more.

The third reason stems from some interpretations of the extraordinary synod of bishops held in 1985, which addressed specific issues relating to the implementation of the Second Vatican Council. Regarding *Dei Verbum*, the bishops expressed some concern that it has not had as broad an effect as is desirable, but they also warned against excesses in interpretation of the council. At the conclusion of the synod, the bishops enumerated in their final report six important principles for the interpretation of Vatican II:[29]

1. We must keep in mind the context of each passage and document as well as how they interrelate.

2. The four constitutions are the essential guide to interpreting the council's other documents.

3. We must not create opposition between the pastoral and doctrinal aspects of the council.

4. We must not separate the spirit and letter of the council from one another.

5. We must respect the continuity of Vatican II with previous councils.

6. Vatican II continues to address the contemporary issues of our day.

Despite some attempts to see these as a way to limit interpretation of the documents of Vatican II, I would affirm the most positive reading of the synod. The principles provide sound guidance for the application of the council's teaching in our own day. The first principle, in fact, calls for keeping the historical context of the council in mind when one seeks to understand its teachings. This is consistent with the historical-critical reading of documents that Vatican II espoused with regard to Scripture. The principles also provide a balanced approach to Vatican II. *Dei Verbum* contains both traditional and innovative elements, and as time goes on, we should not lose sight of both types of elements as we seek to apply its teachings faithfully.

In sum, I think it fair to say that *Dei Verbum*, because of its status as a dogmatic constitution of an ecumenical council—and therefore of the highest authority in church teaching—confirmed and encouraged the direction that has led to a rediscovery of the Bible in Catholic life. One must admit that there have been excesses in interpretation because of the historical-critical method. One such development is the notorious Jesus Seminar. Founded in 1985, this is a voluntary group of scholars who have tried to debunk both church teaching and the historical results of gospel study.[30] Group members do this by voting on whether they deem any particular gospel passage to be historical bedrock tradition or an invention of the early church. The results, needless to say, have been very meager with regard to the former! In the judgment of many scholars, including most Roman Catholic experts, this type of scholarship is an example of the excesses of the historical-critical method. It is not characteristic of most responsible biblical scholarship.

In 1988, (then Cardinal) Joseph Ratzinger, in the context of a symposium in New York City on biblical studies, strongly condemned what he characterized as the excesses of the historical-critical method. He said,

> The historical method can even serve as a cloak for such maneuvers insofar as it dissects the Bible into discontinuous pieces, which are then able to be put to new use and inserted into a new montage (altogether different from the original biblical context).[31]

While some have since taken this to mean that forces set in motion by *Dei Verbum* must be turned around, Ratzinger's position is more nuanced. In interviews at the same symposium, he made observations that were more cautionary. For instance, commenting on the scholarship of Raymond E. Brown, who both during and after his lifetime came under attack by ultraconservatives in the church, Ratzinger said: "I would be very happy if we had many exegetes like Father Brown."[32] Thus, acknowledging the excesses of the historical-critical method does not mean that it is impossible to exercise the method responsibly.

If one rightly points out the excesses of method on the "liberal" side of the question, however, I believe we should also acknowledge excesses on the other end of the ideological spectrum. There is a group of ultra-conservatives who have organized attempts to lobby Rome concerning what they believe is the misinterpretation of *Dei Verbum* and other church teachings. They basically propose that an unnuanced type of inerrancy is at the heart of Catholic teaching and always has been. They have disseminated some of these ideas in an audiotape of a lecture by Professor Brian W. Harrison, OS, titled "Demythologizing the Golden Legend," attacking Raymond E. Brown and others for allegedly distorting the church's teaching on Scripture through the use of the historical-critical method. They even founded a new organization called the International Catholic Council on Biblical Inerrancy (ICCBI) to promote their views. The title clearly indicates the orientation of the group. They seek to reestablish a narrow understanding of biblical inerrancy in the Catholic perspective. In June 2003 they held their first conference in Scranton, Pennsylvania.[33] One does not yet know where this development might lead, but it demonstrates that application and interpretation of *Dei Verbum* is an ongoing struggle.

So, it seems that *Dei Verbum* unwittingly unleashed a firestorm of controversy, at least on questions like biblical inerrancy and the historical-critical method. Unfortunately, *Dei Verbum* is enough of a compromise document that both sides can find some evidence to bolster their stance. In my opinion, however, the excesses that exist on both sides of the aisle on such questions have not won the day, and what we might call the "mainline" interpretation of *Dei Verbum* still holds. In my judgment, the majority of Catholic scholars have judiciously applied the historical-critical method in their scholarship and in their teaching.

As the fortieth anniversary of the constitution approached, conferences were held in various parts of the world to commemorate the constitution's promulgation. Besides the one in Rome sponsored by the Catholic Biblical Federation, mentioned above, another took place in June 2005 in the United States, intended (primarily) for bishops and held at the University of Notre Dame. Various speakers lauded the achievements of the constitution and pointed out challenges that yet remain. At one of his Wednesday audiences in November 2005, Pope Benedict XVI himself drew attention to *Dei Verbum*'s major achievements. He said:

> The conciliar constitution "Dei Verbum" gave an intense impulse to the appreciation of the Word of God, from which has derived a profound renewal of the life of the ecclesial community, above all in preaching, catechesis, theology, spirituality and ecumenical relations.[34]

These words affirm the broad influence the constitution has exercised. They are consistent with the generally positive evaluation of the impact of *Dei Verbum* as the years have gone by. That is as I believe it should be. Despite its limitations, more good has come from the constitution than most of the council fathers may have ever dreamed. This is not to say that the controversy has ended or that there is nothing more for the church to address in its approach to Scripture. On the contrary—but that leads us directly to the next and last part of this book.

PART IV

THE STATE OF THE QUESTIONS

The impact of *Dei Verbum* continues into the third Christian millennium. It so awakened among Catholics the thirst to know more about the Word of God that its effect will be felt for generations. Most scholars would admit that the constitution is not the final word on the matter of divine revelation. But it set forth much of the agenda that has come to the surface since its promulgation. It is no exaggeration to say that the role of the Bible features in almost any current discussion of theological topics, including pastoral and moral issues. In addition, popular American culture has promoted a general interest in biblical "mysteries" that feed public discourse on topics that, in the past, would have been limited to small groups of believers.

In this part of the book we will examine the primary areas where ongoing issues have accrued in the wake of *Dei Verbum*. There are continuing debates among scholars that are an outgrowth of the compromises reflected in the constitution. We will focus on the following:

- the complex relationship of Scripture and Tradition

- the role of the historical-critical method and other methods

- the search for a distinctively "Catholic" approach to biblical interpretation

- the role of the Pontifical Biblical Commission

- the challenges of modern translation of the Bible into English

- the challenges of biblical fundamentalism

SCRIPTURE AND TRADITION

One of the thorniest problems in treating the role of the Bible in the church is to describe how Scripture relates to magisterial Tradition. We pointed out in Part One that this problem became critical after the Protestant Reformation. Protestants adopted a doctrine of "*sola scriptura*," by which was generally meant that the Bible alone provides authoritative teaching for Christian life. The Catholic Church, in reaction to this stance, emphasized the magisterial teaching of the church itself as valid authoritative instruction for Christian life, in addition to Sacred Scripture. We also noted in Part Two that *Dei Verbum* did not entirely resolve the question of how Scripture and Tradition are interrelated. Thus, it is an area of ongoing discussion.

To get at this question we need to discuss three related topics: the authority of Scripture, what is meant by Tradition, and the contemporary debate about the interrelationship of the two.

Authority of Scripture

All Christians claim the Bible to be authoritative because they hold it to be the inspired Word of God. The Bible is unlike any other literature. The writings of St. Augustine or Shakespeare or Milton or John Henry Newman may be inspiring, but they are not inspired. The notion of inspiration comes from the Bible itself. The key passage is found in Second Timothy:

> All scripture is inspired by God and is useful for teaching, for reproof, for correction, and for training in righteousness, so that everyone who belongs to God may be proficient, equipped for every good work. (2 Tim 3:16–17)

The word "inspired" (Greek, *theopneustos*) literally means "God-breathed." That is to say, God breathed life into these words. God is the real author. God's Spirit inhabits Sacred Scripture. Scripture expresses God's will, and thus the Bible has an authority that is unparalleled in any other literature. We should note, however, that the

Greek word does not describe *how* Scripture is inspired. Nor, for that matter, does the passage from Second Timothy resolve the issue. Rather, it asserts that God is the source of the Scriptures' meaning, and they provide sound guidance on how to live a righteous life. Moreover, God's Spirit—the Holy Spirit—is the guarantor of the truth and authenticity of the Bible.

Dei Verbum affirmed this perspective several times.

> For Sacred Scripture is the word of God inasmuch as it is con-signed to writing under the inspiration of the divine Spirit.... (*DV*, 9)

> For holy mother Church...holds that the books of both the Old and New Testaments in their entirety, with all their parts, are sacred and canonical because written under the inspiration of the Holy Spirit, they have God as their author and have been handed on as such to the Church herself. (*DV*, 11)

> Therefore, since everything asserted by the inspired authors or sacred writers must be held to be asserted by the Holy Spirit, it follows that the books of Scripture must be acknowl-edged as teaching solidly, faithfully and without error that truth which God wanted put into sacred writings for the sake of salvation. (*DV*, 11)

These passages from the constitution form a unified stance with regard to the Bible as the inspired Word of God.

How are we to understand God as the "author" of the Bible? The church equally asserts that human authors composed the Scrip-tures "in human fashion" (*DV*, 12), thus requiring interpreters to become aware of the various literary forms and genres represented in the Bible that stem from human origin. Yet inspiration means that the Scriptures contain not merely a human message, but a divine one.

Historically, inspiration has been understood in multiple ways. There are various theories of inspiration, summarized succinctly in the following chart.[1]

THEORY OF INSPIRATION	DESCRIPTION
1. Strict verbal inspiration	Each word of the Bible is inspired; emphasis on the literal reading of Scripture; inspiration connected with inerrancy of the Bible; can apply either to the "original autographs" of the Bible or to translations
2. Limited verbal inspiration	The Scriptures are verbally inspired but in the limited sense of the historical knowledge and cultural context of the biblical authors
3. Inspiration of the content	What is inspired is the meaning or content of each passage of the Bible rather than the words themselves
4. Inspiration of the human authors	The biblical authors were directly inspired by God but chose human words to express their religious experience
5. Inspiration of the early Christian community	Acknowledging the lengthy and complex process by which the Scriptures came into being over centuries, inspiration is imputed to the early Christian community, which ultimately led to the creation of the canon

Each of these theories has advantages and disadvantages. Prior to the twentieth century, most Christians, including Catholics, accepted the first theory of strict verbal inspiration. They thought that inspiration was inherently connected to the notion of inerrancy, meaning that the Bible could contain no errors whatsoever, whether religious, historical, or scientific. Strict biblical fundamentalists still espouse this theory.

In fact, the Catholic position even in the late nineteenth and early twentieth centuries was essentially the same, as reflected in the following quotation from Leo XIII's famous encyclical, *Providentissimus Deus*:

For all the books which the Church receives as sacred and canonical are written wholly and entirely, with all their parts, at the dictation of the Holy Spirit; and so far is it from being possible that any error can coexist with inspiration, that inspiration not only is essentially incompatible with error, but excludes and rejects it as absolutely and necessarily as it is impossible that God Himself, the supreme Truth, can utter that which is not true.

It follows that those who maintain that error is possible in any genuine passage of the sacred writings either pervert the Catholic notion of inspiration or make God the author of such error. (*PD*, 20 and 21)

Such a statement expresses the same position as that of biblical fundamentalists today.

One major problem with this view of inspiration and inerrancy, however, is the inability to decide which text is the inspired one. There are no original "autograph" texts in existence. Rather, there are thousands of manuscript traditions in the original languages (Hebrew, Greek, and Latin). Which manuscript tradition is authoritative? The current editions of the Hebrew Bible, the Greek New Testament, and the Latin Vulgate are all based on scholarly decisions about which families of manuscripts seem to be the most authentic.

This theory raises another question: Does this biblical inspiration apply to translations and not simply to the "originals"? Is the King James Version of the Bible (1611, with subsequent revisions), revered by fundamentalists, the only inspired translation, and, if so, why? These and similar questions make this view of inspiration highly problematic, and it no longer reflects the Catholic stance on inspiration.

The second theory, limited verbal inspiration, is more attuned to a Catholic approach. Even some patristic authors proposed that God accommodated the limitations of the human authors so that the "Word" could be communicated in an understandable fashion. This theory allows for an acknowledgment of the human dimension of the divine text. The biblical text consequently reflects the cultural and linguistic limitations of the authors.

While the third and fourth theories have some potential from a Catholic standpoint, they also have limitations. It is quite difficult to

dict

ascertain either the definitive meaning of texts or the intention of the human authors, and, in either case, the meaning of the words involved is still the critical issue. Many contemporary scholars who are experts in the newer "literary criticism" emphasize that we can never know an ancient author's intentions. Moreover, once a text comes into its existence, it has a life of its own. Regardless of the author's intentions, later readers or generations of readers will elicit meanings from the text that were never in the author's mind but which can legitimately emerge from interpretations of the text.

The fifth theory, proposed by more modern authors of both Protestant and Catholic persuasion, attempts to accommodate the lengthy process of the birth of the biblical tradition in terms of oral, written, and edited (redacted) stages, such as espoused by the PBC's document, *Sancta Mater Ecclesia*. This theory proposes that the real locus of biblical inspiration is not in the Bible itself or in the actual words but in the early communities that preserved these sacred writings and eventually bound them into a restricted collection, the sacred canon, a sure measure or norm for Christian living.

As we saw in Part Two, *Dei Verbum* did not adopt any one theory of inspiration. Neither does the Catechism (*CCC*, 105), which primarily relies on the constitution. The critical passage in *Dei Verbum* is found in article 11, quoted above and repeated here.

> Therefore, since everything asserted by the inspired authors or sacred writers must be held to be asserted by the Holy Spirit, it follows that the books of Scripture must be acknowledged as teaching solidly, faithfully and without error that truth which God wanted put into sacred writings for the sake of salvation. (*DV*, 11)

Some interpreters of the council today insist that this passage essentially affirms the strict verbal inspiration of Scripture, with its concomitant notion of inerrancy, understood literally. Others maintain that this is a misreading of the passage. In fact, as we saw in Part Two, the council fathers rejected using the word "inerrancy" because of its association with biblical fundamentalism. Instead they used "without error" and went on to explain what this expression applies to: "that

_DV 11_

truth which God wanted put into sacred writings for the sake of salvation." This is a crucial passage. The lack of error pertains not to every
jot and tittle of Scripture but to that essential truth necessary for our
salvation. This seems to qualify the type of inspiration found in the
Bible. Inspiration, then, does not concern historical or scientific content but religious content, specifically, moral and doctrinal truths
essential to salvation.

We should, however, issue a note of caution here. In his commentary on this section of the constitution, Cardinal Bea pointed out that
the council fathers did not intend to propose a limited notion of
inerrancy. That is to say, they did not mean to divide inerrancy into
opposing categories of faith versus science or history. He wrote,

> The basic idea of the absolute truth of the Scriptures is always
> the same, although it may be differently expressed. The
> Constitution expresses most forcefully the notion that Scrip-
> ture absolutely guarantees the faithful transmission of God's
> revelation.[2]

He goes on to defend his personal interpretation that the constitution
does not limit inspiration to faith and morals. Yet he does affirm that
the important expression in the constitution concerns the truths essential "for our salvation." In the end, there continues to be a struggle
about how best to understand this notion of inspiration in a manner
that is true to the final form of the constitution but also reflects the
intense debates that led to the compromised wording. Ultimately, I
believe the Catholic position as reflected in _Dei Verbum_ affirms biblical
inspiration wholly but without resolving definitively how it operates
or how best to explain it in detail. The topic will continue to be of
great interest in the future.

Tradition

Perhaps no word is more misunderstood than this one. Many people
think of "tradition" as customs, routine behaviors, or attitudes that
one knew when growing up or have been passed on in a family from

one generation to another. The word "tradition" derives from a Latin word (*tradere*) meaning to "hand down or hand on." The capitalization of the word indicates that, in the sense in which it is used by theologians or in church documents, it does not denote simply "traditions" that accumulate over time. The word "Tradition" means the entire body of teaching and practice in the Judeo-Christian tradition, which is a record of God's covenantal relationship with his chosen people, right down to the beginnings of the church expressed through the apostolic traditions recounted in the Bible and beyond.

This is indeed a very large, all-encompassing notion. It includes thousands of years of the history of salvation and of the relationship between God and all creation, most specifically with human beings, who are created in God's own image (Genesis 1–2). The biblical sense of the word "tradition" denotes both a *process* of handing on truth from one generation to another and the *content* of that truth. For example, St. Paul speaks of handing on traditions about the Eucharist (1 Cor 11:23–26) and the resurrection of Jesus (1 Cor 15:3–11). These are not merely minor rituals but vitally important remembrances. The process of handing on these truths was as important as the message they contained.

In a pre-Vatican II setting, Tradition came to denote primarily a body of authoritative teachings, apart from Scripture, that contained the truths of the Catholic faith. When the popes of the nineteenth century began to issue "encyclical letters," which were intended as authoritative teachings in their own right, this practice reinforced the content-oriented notion of Tradition. In contrast, as we noted in Part Two, *Dei Verbum* proposed a more dynamic understanding of Tradition.

> Therefore the Apostles, handing on what they themselves had received, warn the faithful to hold fast to the traditions which they have learned either by word of mouth or by letter (see 2 Thess. 2:15), and to fight in defense of the faith handed on once and for all (see Jude 1:3). Now what was handed on by the Apostles includes everything which contributes toward the holiness of life and increase in faith of the peoples of God; and so the Church, in her teaching, life and worship, perpetuates

and hands on to all generations all that she herself is, all that she believes.

This tradition which comes from the Apostles develops in the Church with the help of the Holy Spirit. *For there is a growth in the understanding of the realities and the words which have been handed down.* This happens through the contemplation and study made by believers, who treasure these things in their hearts (see Luke, 2:19, 51) through a penetrating understanding of the spiritual realities which they experience, and through the preaching of those who have received through episcopal succession the sure gift of truth. For as the centuries succeed one another, the Church constantly moves forward toward the fullness of divine truth until the words of God reach their complete fulfillment in her. (*DV*, 8; emphasis added)

The highlighted words express the dynamism of the church's Tradition as it proceeds through the ages. These words hark back to the notion of John XXIII at the beginning of the council that the expression of the truths of the faith is different from the truths themselves. Every era must wrestle with how best to communicate the truth contained in the Tradition of the church in ways that make it understandable and more attractive to people.

Cardinal Bea, in his thorough commentary on *Dei Verbum*, explains this concept in a helpful manner. After acknowledging the seemingly paradoxical expression of "developing tradition," he states: "The development of tradition consists of an ever growing understanding of its object, in its entirety."[3] It is not a question of a totally new revelation that comes into existence in this developing tradition. Rather, the comprehension and depth of awareness of God's self-revelation can deepen over time.

Tradition, then, is more than doctrines, teachings, formal pronouncements, and the like, although magisterial teachings are clearly among its essential elements. Tradition embraces the living practices of the community of faith, as well as the biblical history that led to the birth of the church.

Relating Scripture and Tradition

After the Reformation, the division between Scripture and Tradition became more solidified. Protestants thus emphasized one source of divine revelation (Scripture), while Catholics emphasized two inter-related expressions of one source (Scripture and Tradition).

Just as Vatican II rejected the propositional view of revelation, so it rejected a proposal to affirm two separate sources of revelation. The pertinent section of *Dei Verbum* (article 9) was, in fact, much debated, as we saw in Part Two. When the council fathers rejected the first schema's attempt to delineate two sources of revelation, the real challenge became how to express the interrelationship of Scripture and Tradition. This is a part of the constitution that many find unsatisfying, because it does not offer a clear resolution to the question (*DV*, 9 and 10).

Again, Cardinal Bea's explanation is helpful. He points out that "the document does not say that the sacred writings are understood *only* in light of tradition."[4] Nor does the constitution say "...that tradition is necessary for the deeper understanding of scripture."[5] Tradition can help bring greater clarity to the interpretation of Scripture because the sum total of Tradition (i.e., devotion, liturgical practice, meditation, study, and so on) helps focus on the meaning of the text in different eras of the church's history. The meaning of the Scriptures, then, is not self-evident. It is not immediately transparent to any casual interpreter. Careful exegesis (the formal term for getting at the meaning of texts) is required to ascertain, first, the literal sense of the words, and then second, deeper meanings that are contained therein. The church promotes this exercise of interpretation in the context of its whole living Tradition.

We should also remember that it was the Tradition of the church that helped bring the canon of Sacred Scripture into being. There is, in a sense, a back-and-forth relationship between Scripture and Tradition. On the one hand, Scripture is a special gift from God, through the Holy Spirit, that instructs us and reveals God's intentions. But the Bible did not just descend miraculously from heaven. It grew from the experience of our ancestors in faith. On the other hand, the church itself determined, under the guidance of the Holy Spirit, the extent of the Scriptures. Scripture and Tradition thus involve a dialectical relationship. The church, under the guidance of the Holy Spirit, defined the extent of the canon and determined which books were acceptable and which were not. This was a long and complex process that went on for centuries. It did not reach a definitive conclusion until the Council of Trent in the sixteenth century, when the limits of the canon were formally confirmed.[6]

Commenting on this hazy relationship, Cardinal Bea notes that the council fathers left the formulation rather broad for the following reason:

> The Council wished to emphasize the fundamental impor-tance of tradition, without however deciding the question which Catholics still debate on the so-called 'sufficiency of Holy Scripture', whether, that is to say, all revealed truths are at least implicitly contained in the written word of God, or whether on the contrary, some of them are received by the Church from oral tradition alone.[7]

This is to say that the mysterious interrelationship between Scripture and Tradition is not resolved in the constitution, and scholars con-tinue to debate the issue. What is clear, however, is that Scripture and Tradition continue to inform one another. There is a back-and-forth, a give-and-take kind of relationship that allows the Scriptures to better challenge the church to the vision its Savior, Jesus Christ, the incarnate Word, imparted to the apostles. After all, *Dei Verbum* strongly cautioned that the church is the servant— not the master—of the Scriptures: "This teaching office is not above the word of God, but serves it, ..." (*DV*, 10). But there is also the function of the entire Tradition of the church to help guide our understanding of Scripture through the ages, beginning with but not restricted to the apostolic preaching. This dialectic is not likely to be entirely clarified, though continued reflection will doubtless lead to a deeper understanding of this mystery.

I realize that this topic is very complex and may cause confusion. In an attempt to help readers visualize this elusive relationship of Scripture, Tradition, and the magisterial teaching of the church, I offer the following diagram and an explanation rooted in article 10 of the constitution.

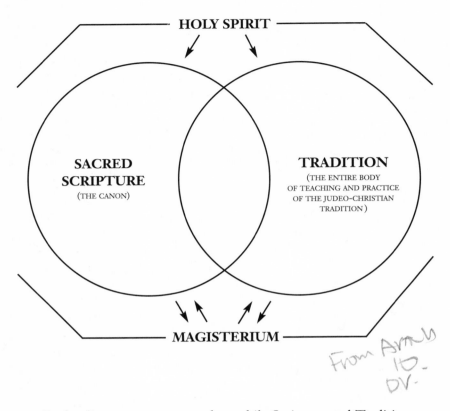

In the diagram one can see that, while Scripture and Tradition are distinctive entities, they overlap. The Holy Spirit is equally active in both of these spheres because, in reality, they constitute one divine source of revelation. The magisterium, seemingly a third entity, has its own distinctive role to play. In some ways, the magisterium stands apart from the Tradition of the church, yet it is also an essential part of the Tradition. *Dei Verbum* notes that the magisterium's exclusive role is to ensure, under the guidance of the Holy Spirit, the authentic interpretation of the Word of God. But the "living teaching office of the Church" is also the bearer of the Tradition of the church. Ultimately, then, the magisterium helps to interpret both Scripture and Tradition authentically, "in the name of Jesus Christ" (arrows pointing upward). Yet *Dei Verbum* equally stresses that the magisterium does not stand above the Word of God but serves it (arrows pointing downward). The magisterium itself can be corrected by insights from Scripture and Tradition. God directs the efficacy of all three entities under the Holy Spirit (arrows pointing downward). The constitution concludes its discussion of this complex relationship with the following summary:

> It is clear, therefore, that sacred tradition, Sacred Scripture and the teaching authority of the Church, in accord with God's most wise design, are so linked and joined together that one cannot stand without the others, and that all together and each in its own way under the action of the one Holy Spirit contribute effectively to the salvation of souls (*DV*, 10).

There is, of course, a problem that some would see with this scenario. They would note that the magisterium's role has seemingly grown so much that there seems to be little control over it, despite the constitution's insistence that it is "not above the Word of God, but serves it" (*DV*, 10). Some council fathers foresaw this problem and expressed uneasiness with it, even during the discussions of article 10. They felt that *Dei Verbum* did not say enough about the role of the Word in supervising the teaching office of the church itself.

Christopher Butler, for example, at an ecumenical conference held in 1966 to examine the teachings of Vatican II, voiced his concern with these words:

> It is all very well for us to say and believe that the magisterium is subject to Holy Scripture. But is there anybody who is in a position to tell the magisterium: Look, you are not practicing your subjection to Scripture in your teaching.[8]

Such sentiments harmonize well with concerns expressed by some theologians and others in recent years that the teaching office of the church has grown more authoritarian. They believe that the magisterium needs once more to root itself in the teaching of *Dei Verbum*, but one has to admit that the constitution is not as clear on the subject as one might like. There is essentially a paradox here. John R. Donahue summarizes it in these words:

Thus the teaching office is simultaneously the servant of the
Word and its authentic interpreter; the whole Church deter-
mines the development of tradition, but is subordinate to the
teaching authority.[9]

If the constitution did not definitively resolve this complex relationship, it nonetheless laid an important foundation for future discussions
of the matter.

THE HISTORICAL-CRITICAL METHOD AND OTHER METHODS

Because much of the controversy about methodology in Scripture
since Vatican II has centered on the historical-critical method, we
need now to examine the nature of criticisms leveled against this
method and evaluate their validity in more depth. But we begin with a
few general observations.[10]

The historical-critical method should be placed first in its historical context. It grew primarily out of nineteenth-century academic circles
in which scholars began to analyze the Scriptures with an eye toward
verifying the historical content of the Bible. The word "criticism" does
not, however, mean that the method "criticizes" the Bible. Rather, the
word translates a German word that really means a "scientific study."
Thus, this method uses scientific and linguistic tools to test the literal
accuracy of the biblical books. Often the results of this scholarship did
lead to conclusions that were, in fact, highly critical of the historical
data in the Bible. Yet many times scholars also found what they
thought could be judged to be "historical bedrock" in the Bible.
Methodologically, the emphasis has been on the use of scientific tools
to reach accurate, trustworthy conclusions.

A second point to remember is that the historical-critical method
actually is a set of methods, not one uniform approach. Although it is
a "diachronic" method, i.e., it focuses on texts throughout their history, there are multiple aspects to it. Indeed, there has been growth in
the use of scientific tools for scholarly biblical studies over the course
of the last two centuries. There are great differences of approach
between form, source, and redaction criticisms, for instance, even
though all three are part of the "historical-critical" method. Form

Redaction.

criticism concentrates on the search for the oral traditions that lie behind the biblical data. Source criticism is interested in identifying the sources, both oral and literary, that the biblical authors may have used to shape their books. Redaction criticism, on the other hand, focuses on theological emphases that can be discerned in various interrelated biblical books, such as the Gospels. Yet all three are exemplary of the historical-critical approach to Scripture. All three have an interest in delineating the historical parameters of the biblical books. When critics assail the historical-critical method, it is because of alleged interrelated failures on the part of the practitioners of the historical-critical method in general, rather than the limitations of any one of the various methods it comprises.

Finally, there are positive contributions that have been made by historical-criticism to the life of the church. The PBC goes so far as to say, "The historical-critical method is the indispensable method for scientific study of the meaning of ancient texts" (*IBC*, §I.A.). It adds some evaluative statements regarding this method. Essentially, the commission sees three values in the method. First, if it is used "in an objective manner," it precludes *a priori* biases that can interfere with objective interpretation. Second, its orientation toward the sources of biblical texts has provided "fresh access to the Bible," especially regarding its literary and historical background. Finally, it has led to a proper emphasis on the "literal sense" of Scripture as a beginning for further reflection on the text. One must always deal with the actual words and genre of the text in order to probe deeper into its meaning. Spiritual meanings do not emerge independent of the literal meaning of the words but are intimately connected to it.

To these I would add another contribution. Most important, as pointed out in Part Three, the historical-critical method has enabled the Roman Catholic Church to enter into ecumenical dialogue in a far more sophisticated manner than was ever possible prior to Vatican II. With the encouragement of *Divino Afflante Spiritu* and *Dei Verbum*, Catholic scholars quickly became adept at applying the historical-critical method to biblical interpretation in ways that allowed open and honest dialogue on an equal footing with Protestant scholars to take place. This was no minor achievement. It enhanced one of the most apparent goals of Vatican II itself, namely, to be an ecumenical council.

Despite these positive values, there are limitations to and criticisms of the method. We now turn to these.

Eight Criticisms of the Historical-Critical Method

First, critics point out that all too often the historical-critical method has become for its practitioners *the* only method of approach to the Bible.[11] They believe that there is a certain tyranny of approach that historical-critical exegetes have forced on the general public, to the detriment of any other approach.

A second criticism is that in their approach historical critics assume a pristine, scientific, external objectivity that simply does not exist. The fact is that no one is immune to biases. For example, such factors as one's gender, ethnicity, or level of education can dictate how one approaches the Bible and what questions one asks of it. Even the best exegetes have limitations of approach and perspective that should be acknowledged. There is always a danger in biblical exegesis that each interpreter can see in the text what he or she wants to see. This can lead to eisegesis (reading into a text something that is not there) rather than exegesis. Critics of the method believe that practitioners too often deny or ignore these biases.

Third, critics believe that historical criticism, as its name would imply, is overly obsessed with questions of history. Seeking bedrock historical facts or ascertaining where theological accretions may have appeared in the biblical text, they insist, always seems to take precedence to any other approach, and this imposes a serious limitation on the results of biblical criticism. In fact, since the time of the Enlightenment, there has been an obsession among modern people to determine the "facts" of the Bible. Scholars have explored the miracle stories of the Gospels, for instance, to try to determine "what really happened."

A corollary and fourth criticism is that practitioners ignore or neglect other well-established approaches to the Bible, especially those that emphasize the deeper meanings of Scripture. Historical critics allegedly have no openness to deeper meanings, among them the spiritual meaning of Sacred Scripture, which goes back to the most ancient traditions of biblical interpretation.

Fifth, practitioners have seriously neglected the longstanding and ancient contribution of patristic-era interpreters. Many of the early church fathers wrote extensive commentaries on virtually all the biblical books. Modern exegetes, the critics contend, ignore the commentaries of great interpreters like Origen, St. Jerome, St. Augustine, St. John Chrysostom, and many others who wrote insightful but pre-scientific interpretations of the Bible. Allegedly, these materials are passed over because they are judged to be non-scientific and highly imaginative readings of Scripture, and therefore of less interest for historical questions.

A sixth criticism focuses on the emphasis of the historical-critical method on the sources of the biblical books. This criticism encompasses two dimensions. One is that the hyper-interest in source questions leads to an endless number of hypothetical scholarly theories about supposed sources. Examples could abound, but the highly complex Documentary Hypothesis about the origins of the Pentateuch and the Modified Two-Source Hypothesis of the four Gospels are cases in point. Another dimension of this criticism is that even methods such as redaction criticism lead to such over-indulgence in source hypotheses. Although redaction criticism is ostensibly interested in the "theological" tendencies of a book, historical critics often have to hypothesize how the biblical author modified his alleged sources in order to arrive at what his theological emphases may have been. Thus, in two ways, historical criticism overemphasizes source questions to the detriment of deeper, theological or spiritual interpretations.

Seventh, and perhaps the most serious criticism of modern scientific exegesis, is that its excessive historical skepticism has led to an erosion of faith, especially among laity in the church. When non-specialists learn, for instance, that the Genesis story of creation (Genesis 1–3) was not meant to be taken literally, or that Jesus' miracle of the multiplication of the loaves did not necessarily happen exactly as it is narrated multiple times in the Gospels (e.g., Mark 6:34–44 and 8:1–9), these revelations can dishearten them. Moreover, critics believe that historical-critical interpretation has led to a devaluation of doctrinal aspects of Scripture. They add that exegetes themselves have emphasized historicism and rationalism and put an anti-dogmatic spin on their task as biblical interpreters in such a way as to oppose a valid faith dimension to interpretation.

Finally, there is a small but vocal group of ultraconservative critics who have waged a relentless campaign against the historical-critical method on the basis that its alleged acceptance by Vatican Council II is actually a misinterpretation of the council. Some of these critics have questionable academic credentials; others have professional training but have conducted a virulent attack upon those whom they perceive to be the key promoters of the historical-critical method. Most frequently, Raymond E. Brown (1928–1998), a Sulpician scripture scholar whose prolific works contributed greatly to the spread of Scripture study among Catholics after the council, was a target of these attacks. Even seven years and more after his death, some critics are still waging a campaign against his name.

These eight criticisms, of course, are not all of equal weight. Nor are they necessarily proposed only by ultraconservatives in the church. Moderate voices, too, have expressed concerns about the historical-critical method, especially in recent years. All the criticisms deserve a careful assessment, since they impinge upon the legacy of *Dei Verbum*. It should also be noted that, *a fortiori*, those who hesitate to apply historical-critical analysis to the Bible are just as reluctant to apply it to *Dei Verbum* itself, or to any other church teaching. Yet we saw in Part One that the constitution was born out of much discussion and no little compromise.

Evaluating the Criticisms

If one weeds out the excessively strident and irrational criticisms, there are nonetheless some limitations to the historical-critical method that are legitimate.

With regard to the first criticism, there have been some scholars since Vatican II who have perhaps made historical criticism the only method in their arsenal of exegetical tools, but they would be few in number. It is true that modern exegetes from the nineteenth and twentieth centuries have been often preoccupied with historical issues. However, since the 1980s, in particular, no reputable scholar could afford to ignore the proliferation of new methodologies and approaches to biblical interpretation that go beyond the historical-critical method.

Just to name a few of these new methods: rhetorical criticism, composition criticism, narrative criticism, reader-response criticism, semiotics, social-scientific criticism, feminist interpretation, liberation-oriented interpretation, and a host of others. Many of these are explicitly non-historical in orientation. They are "synchronic" rather than diachronic in design, since they focus on the text itself and not the underlying historical context. In fact, a few of them are almost anti-historical, emphasizing that once texts come into existence, they bear a life of their own, apart from their historical origins. No scholar can ignore this explosion of methodologies, even though it would be impossible for any one scholar to master all of them. As the PBC's document *The Interpretation of the Bible in the Church* indicates, *every* method comes with strengths and weaknesses. All modern methods, including the historical-critical method, have made an important contribution to biblical studies. And, as we have pointed out before, the PBC's instruction did insist that the historical-critical method is "indispensable" to plumb the meaning of ancient texts (*IBC*, §I.A). So a contemporary challenge is how to utilize these various methods, in conjunction with historical criticism, to the benefit of the interpretive enterprise.

The second criticism contains some truth as well. No doubt some historical critics touted the results of their scientific investigations of Scripture as strictly objective. This claim is exaggerated. It implies that anyone who approaches interpretation from a scientific perspective is objective while someone using a faith perspective is not. This dichotomy is false. While there may be some scholars situated in academic settings who take such a position, it is not predominant. Most scholars today recognize their biases in interpretation and are willing to admit them. Indeed, many professional commentators on the Bible state boldly their faith (or denominational) perspective as a feature of their interpretation. They nonetheless attempt to maintain as objective a stance as they can in their work of interpretation.

The third criticism is a little more difficult to evaluate. By definition, historical criticism is interested in historical questions. Realizing that prior to the Enlightenment the Bible's historicity was simply presumed, it was only natural that modern scientific methods would begin to probe heretofore unknown historical dimensions of the Scriptures. That such historical positivism sometimes reigned supreme among biblical scholars is no doubt true. But most Roman Catholic biblical scholars see themselves as being at the service of the church. Historical knowledge is not the only value that comes from biblical interpretation, for the religious meaning is, in fact, more important. Scholars are engaged in the larger enterprise of biblical interpretation, which includes a dialogue of faith.

The fourth and fifth criticisms can be addressed together. While some historical critics, in their preoccupation with historical questions, have ignored other aspects of interpretation, such as spiritual meaning or patristic insights, that cannot be said of most. Many major commentaries by Roman Catholic scholars contain references to patristic interpreters and plumb the spiritual meaning of passages, in addition to assessing historical questions. The enduring popularity of Raymond E. Brown's two-volume commentary on John's Gospel, for instance, is not due solely to its historical value. Many preachers continue to find in it profound insights that are helpful in preaching on that Gospel. Moreover, commentaries have now appeared that utilize more directly patristic interpretations or that emphasize the spiritual message of the biblical books.[12] Most of these are written by trained historical critics who nevertheless are able to blend their scientific approach with more spiritual interests.

The sixth criticism, in my opinion, is somewhat on target. The fact is that scholars have written a plethora of books and articles on hypotheses about sources that have proven to be mind-boggling. Let me cite one example.

Scholars have long proposed the existence of a pre-Marcan passion narrative (Mark 14–15) that narrates the story of Jesus' passion and death. In his monumental study of the passion, *The Death of the Messiah*, Raymond E. Brown included an appendix from one of his former students, Professor Marion L. Soards, which reviewed these many hypotheses.[13] In fact, he carefully examined thirty-five different scholarly proposals on what such a pre-Marcan passion narrative might have looked like. At the end of this exhaustive study, Soards concludes:

> Our investigation brings us thus to a positive conclusion and a point of challenge. We may safely conclude that Mark uses a source in writing his P[assion] N[arrative]. We know that source,

however, only as incorporated in Mark. The greatest challenge that lies before us is not the separation of tradition from Marcan redaction; for, as our earlier work shows, that task may finally be an impossible one. Rather, we must investigate the rich layers of traditions that come to us in the form of the Marcan P[assion] N[arrative].

Soards's conclusion, I think, is a just one. How does such a large number of hypothetical proposals about the possible underlying traditions of the Gospels help the average Bible reader understand the text better?

Such a bewildering number of hypotheses is bound to cause great confusion. This excessive desire to recreate what lies *behind* the biblical text, with endless hypotheses, does little to instill confidence in lay readers of ever discerning the *meaning* of the text. As Soards notes, this is likely an "impossible" task. A profusion of confusing hypotheses, which actually yield meager secure results, has understandably led people to distrust the excesses of the historical-critical method. This is not to suggest that scholars should cease all such activity. Rather, balance is needed. That is why other exegetical methods have returned to examining the biblical text as it exists.

The seventh criticism also expresses some justifiable concerns. There are people who feel that their faith has been severely shaken by the historical skepticism that often accompanies the historical-critical method. Some cavalier professors no doubt enjoy tossing out critical observations for the sheer value of shocking their audience. The tale is told of a biblical professor who was giving a public lecture that clearly upset at least one member of the audience who complained that her faith was being destroyed by his lecture. He reportedly responded, "Well, that's the price of progress!" Whether this story is apocryphal or not, I believe it is an excess not frequently encountered among responsible scholars. Most Catholic scholars that I know freely accept the necessity of interpreting the Bible within a faith context. Modern historical methods are not opposed to faith—nor do they destroy faith. On the contrary, they put the faith on more solid ground. They root the biblical doctrines in scientific observations that can help open up the meanings of texts in their historical contexts.

Finally, the last criticism we have noted deserves some comment. A small but vocal, and at times influential, group of ultraconservatives in the church continue to wage a kind of guerilla warfare against modern, scientific study of the Bible. Some of their destructive and mean-spirited attacks on good, faithful Catholic scholars have been recounted in great detail and need not be repeated here.[14] All that I can say is that I believe this group operates out of excessive fear and does little to promote sound biblical interpretation. They will doubtless linger indefinitely on the horizon, for they are convinced of the rightfulness of their position. That position has little to commend it and does not warrant an extensive response.

What, then, can we say about the value of the historical-critical method? A balanced approach to it will recognize the solid contribution it makes to the life of the church by promoting generally sound biblical interpretation. Joseph Ratzinger (now Pope Benedict XVI), who at the time of the council was an important young theologian, wrote:

> Even now, after the Council, it is not possible to say that the question of the relation between critical and Church exegesis, historical research and dogmatic tradition has been settled. All that is certain is that from now on it will be impossible to ignore the critical historical method and that, precisely as such, it is in accordance with the aims of theology itself.[15]

At times, however, historical criticism has exercised a domineering position that has overshadowed other useful approaches to biblical interpretation. At other times, it has led to excesses in scholarly method, such as overly skeptical results and a freewheeling, anti-institutional approach that has alarmed some of the faithful and done harm to their faith. Furthermore, if biblical exegesis were to be primarily left to professional exegetes in secular university settings, there is a danger that biblical scholarship might be exercised strictly apart from a faith perspective, calling into question the church's role in biblical interpretation. This need not be the case. Historical criticism need not be opposed to a faith perspective. Neither do I believe that the church can ever afford to ignore the historical-critical method. One of the lasting legacies of *Dei Verbum* surely is its fostering of this method, in conjunction with other methods, as a "window" into the biblical world. With judicious application, the historical-critical method will last well into the third millennium and interact with other methodologies currently flourishing and those yet to arrive on the scene.

In conclusion, methodology will certainly be a central focus of biblical studies into the future. Scholars continue to invent new approaches to the Scriptures, approaches that go far beyond the historical-critical method. Many of them are self-described "postmodern" methods that supposedly move beyond the historical orientation of the nineteenth and twentieth centuries.[16] These scholars often emphasize the independent life of texts, noting that, once they have come into being, one can find in them meanings that may not have been intended by the authors. Indeed, there are scholars who insist that neither historical context nor authorial intention has anything to do with the interpretation of a text. Some methodologies offer highly fanciful interpretations of biblical texts. Some are clearly anti–faith oriented and attempt to "deconstruct" traditional approaches to interpretation in order to get at a "pristine" interpretation not influenced by the alleged overlays of church interpretation. The work of the famous "Jesus Seminar," which we mentioned in Part Three, moves in this direction. Finally, there is also a trend to rediscover the value of patristic and medieval interpretations that have often been eclipsed in modern times.

We should also remember in this discussion that the PBC has recommended that most methods or interpretative approaches to Scripture have pros and cons to them. The PBC noted that even feminist interpretation or approaches characterized by liberation perspectives have made useful contributions to our understanding of biblical passages (*IBC*, §I.E).[17] But sometimes preconceived ideological stances dictate more what one wants to see in the Bible than what is actually there. That is ever the danger in exegesis and interpretation. Yet, carefully practiced, most methods do contribute to the fund of knowledge about the Bible that can nourish present and future generations of Christians.

The point here is to see that method in biblical studies continues to be a focus of attention. *Dei Verbum* helped set in motion modern Catholic study of the Bible, but it did not offer a definitive direction for the future. For that, the church will have to encourage its experts to use all their skill and knowledge to move the discussion forward wherever it may lead, under the watchful guidance of church authorities who, in Catholic practice, have the serious obligation of guiding authentic interpretation with the aid of the Holy Spirit.

3. THE SEARCH FOR A "CATHOLIC" APPROACH TO INTERPRETATION

The controversies over methodology have more recently led to a scholarly discussion of whether one can legitimately ascribe to Catholicism a distinctive, if not necessarily unique, approach to biblical interpretation. The reasons for this are multiple. In the first place, there is considerable dissatisfaction among scholars about the predominance of the historical method that we have just treated above at length. Second, there is concern over the explosion of new methods in biblical studies that continue to appear at a phenomenal rate. And finally, there is a certain nostalgia for previous methods of biblical interpretation, especially patristic methods, which have sometimes been obscured by modern preoccupations. All of these are legitimate concerns. But where is the discussion leading us?

The entire issue of what constitutes a distinctively Catholic approach to the Bible emerged as a scholarly topic of conversation in the late 1990s. The primary reason for this was dissatisfaction with the dominance of the historical-critical method and a desire to reclaim past approaches to Scripture (e.g., patristic interpretation, *lectio divina*, and so on).

Professor Luke Timothy Johnson voiced a strong cry for this search in an address to the Catholic Biblical Association at its annual meeting in August 1997.[18] His talk, titled "What's Catholic about Catholic Biblical Scholarship?" roused strong feelings from the audience and precipitated a scholarly debate that continues to the present. Johnson basically stated that too many Catholic exegetes had allowed the historical-critical method, which grew out of a Protestant environment, to ignore or even belittle the traditional "pre-critical" types of exegesis that are a part of the Catholic heritage.

Johnson's salvo was quickly met by one of the great names of modern Catholic biblical studies, Roland E. Murphy, who defended the use of the historical-critical method and located the Catholic character of exegesis in the person of the interpreter of Scripture, rather than in any method.[19]

One author who has done extensive work on this question, Peter S. Williamson, has proposed that there are at least twenty principles that make up a Catholic approach to Scripture.[20] He bases his argument on the PBC's 1993 document, *The Interpretation of the Bible in the Church*, which he believes contains the main elements of a Catholic approach to the Bible, even though that was not the primary intention of the commission. He groups the twenty principles into six categories, as follows.

A. The foundational principle
   1. The Word of God is communicated in human words; thus the message comes both from God and the inspired human authors.

B. Catholic exegesis and scientific method
   2. Because the Bible is expressed in human words, Catholic exegetes freely use scientific methods, as objectively as possible, to discern its meaning.
   3. Because revelation takes place in history, Catholic interpretation always considers the historical dimensions of the text.
   4. Because the Bible is literature, Catholic exegetes use philological and literary tools to interpret it.
   5. Catholic exegetes also use philosophical hermeneutics to explore the sacred texts.

C. Catholic exegesis and the Christian faith
   6. Catholic exegetes recognize that human reason alone cannot suffice for biblical interpretation; they rely also on the Holy Spirit to be their interpretive guide.
   7. The believing community also plays a role in interpretation, because the Scriptures belong to the whole church.
   8. Catholic interpretation recognizes the essential unity in Scripture and seeks to interpret Scripture within this discernible pattern.
   9. Catholics emphasize the interrelationship between the Old and New Testaments, especially noting that the New Testament interprets and sheds light on the Old.

10. Biblical interpretation in the Catholic tradition recognizes the living tradition of the church, especially the contribution of the patristic era, in interpreting Scripture.
11. The main goal of Catholic interpretation is to get at the religious message contained in the Bible.

D. The meaning of inspired Scripture
12. The literal sense of the Scriptures, expressed by the human words, is the beginning of exegesis, but the words allow for broader and deeper understandings to unfold through history.
13. The spiritual sense of Scripture, which is rooted in the literal sense, is the meaning expressed by the Holy Spirit; typological interpretation (recognition of "types" in the Bible) is an important aspect of this sense.
14. Catholic exegetes also recognize a deeper or fuller sense of Scripture (Latin, *sensus plenior*), intended by God but not clearly expressed by the human authors.

E. Methods and approaches
15. Catholic exegetes use the historical-critical method as an indispensable tool, but its limitations are acknowledged.
16. No one method characterizes Catholic biblical interpretation; all methods have strengths and weaknesses.

F. Interpretation in practice
17. Catholic exegetes determine as accurately as possible the meaning of Scripture and bring it into dialogue with other disciplines (e.g., theology, prayer) that enhance the life of the church.
18. Catholic exegesis recognizes the ability of the Scriptures to be "actualized" anew age after age, thus allowing for new insights to come forth.
19. The Word of God transcends the culture(s) into which it was born and interacts with contemporary cultures to produce new meanings.
20. Authentic interpretation occurs in the life of the church in the multiple ways—such as liturgy, *lectio divina*, pastoral ministry, and ecumenism—in which the church uses the Word of God.

This is an incredibly rich listing of principles, which many would acknowledge do flow from the PBC's document. Williamson's approach has much to commend it, but one might raise questions about it. For instance, many of the distinctive "Catholic" principles he enunciates would overlap with other approaches, whether Protestant or Jewish. Moreover, many believing Christians would interpret Scripture within a faith framework and would not rely exclusively on a scientific, historical analysis. It is too early to tell whether Williamson's proposal will hold up long-term under scrutiny, but at least he has become an important partner in the conversation.

Other scholars propose that the distinctive Catholic element of biblical interpretation is embedded in a doctrinal exposition of Scripture. For example, William S. Kurz has suggested one can properly read Scripture through the optic of the Nicene Creed or the church's teaching on the sanctity of human life or on the sacraments.[21] An acknowledged danger in this approach is eisegesis, reading into the text something that is not there. Such doctrinal approaches must carefully discern between the seeds of certain doctrines that may rightfully be rooted in Scripture and later doctrinal developments that go beyond the Scriptures themselves.

Another approach is represented by the concept of the paschal mystery. Two scholars have proposed that this notion of the total work of Christ seen in the Scriptures and in the life of the church is what makes a Catholic understanding of Scripture distinctive.[22] They suggest that all Scripture must be interpreted through this hermeneutical principle if it is to represent a faithful approach to biblical interpretation. Others would question whether such an external, hermeneutical concept is really adequate as an approach to Scripture. They argue that such an approach imposes on the process of interpretation an artificial category that, in the end, does a grave injustice to biblical exegesis.

All of this discussion, in my judgment, should be placed in the context of the PBC's warning, in *The Interpretation of the Bible in the Church*: "Catholic exegesis does not claim any particular scientific method as its own" (*IBC*, §III). What is helpful in the PBC's instruction is the acknowledgment that Catholic interpretation respects the continuing ability of Sacred Scripture to foster new readings or "re-readings" (French, *relectures*) of passages. In every age, there is the

possibility of new and refreshing insights that lead to novel understandings of specific passages. Some of these may emerge because of
new methods of interpretation and new questions being asked of the
text. Newer understandings might also arise from a review of ancient
interpretations that now, in a new context, might lead to a fresh
understanding. That is why a Catholic approach must be truly "catholic," i.e., universal, embracing all different types of exegetical method
that can be useful.

Invoking principles from *Dei Verbum*, the PBC document also
highlights the process of "actualization" of Scripture, by which new
circumstances and contexts can lead to new interpretations of familiar
biblical passages (*IBC*, §IV.A.1). Citing the fact that the Bible itself uti-
lizes this approach (e.g., New Testament use of Old Testament passages), the commission emphasizes several principles:

- The ability to "actualize" Scripture is due to the richness
  and depth of meaning within the Bible.

- Actualization requires careful interpretative application to
  modern contexts (technically, hermeneutics) precisely because
  the Bible has eternal value.

- Actualization requires attention to the complex interrelationship of the Old and New Testaments.

- Actualization must take place within the living Tradition of
  the church.

- Actualization should never mean manipulation of the text
  but objective interpretation.

These principles, in fact, reflect the approach espoused by *Dei Verbum*
(especially in articles 10–13). Catholic interpretation always takes
place within the larger context of a living Tradition. The issue, then, is
not primarily which method or set of methods characterizes Catholic
interpretation, but in what larger context biblical interpretation takes
place.

From this summary, one easily sees that this question of what constitutes a truly "Catholic" approach to Scripture has touched a nerve.
Perhaps there is something essential about Catholic identity more

than forty years after *Dei Verbum* that makes this question so urgent. The issue, in fact, goes far beyond anything envisioned in the constitution, and it is timely and important and worthy of serious discussion. When this issue is coupled with the dissatisfaction over the historical-critical method treated above, I suspect the discussion will continue well into the future and will not easily be resolved.

4. THE PONTIFICAL BIBLICAL COMMISSION

The Pontifical Biblical Commission is at the center of one aspect of ongoing controversies about a Catholic approach to Scripture within the church since *Dei Verbum*. There are those who say that the PBC has no magisterial authority to teach about Scripture since Paul VI downgraded it to a consultative body of the Congregation for the Doctrine of the Faith. Others maintain that the PBC's documents, when issued with papal approval, are in fact part of authoritative Catholic teaching on the Bible. We need to examine this question carefully. Both sides have a point, but the situation is more complex than some would wish.

Pope Leo XIII established the PBC by means of an apostolic letter titled *Vigilantiae* on October 30, 1902. The historical context for this move was the Modernist crisis that alarmed the church in the late nineteenth century. In the wake of exaggerated historical skepticism by some interpreters of the Bible, Leo wanted to bolster his own encyclical, *Providentissimus Deus* (1893), which we discussed earlier. It had demonstrated both his concerns about some modern trends in biblical interpretation and his openness to responsible, scientific biblical scholarship. The PBC essentially gave the church an organ that could guide biblical interpretation through turbulent times.

Leo's brief apostolic letter set forth the structure and purpose of the PBC. It was to consist of a number of cardinals (twenty) who would be assisted by a small body of consultors. The pope would appoint these consultors from different countries according to their recognized competency as biblical scholars. The PBC would meet in Rome, under the watchful eye of the pope himself, and Leo noted that he would establish a part of the Vatican Library for the commission's use. He also promised to enlarge the library's holdings in manuscripts, and the like, to ensure that the commission had the best resources at hand for their work.

The purpose of the PBC is also instructive. *Vigilantiae* (as the title would suggest) emphasized the need for bishops to watch over scriptural studies carefully because some of the concerns expressed in *Providentissimus Deus* remained prevalent. Thus the PBC was to ensure that "... the divine text will find here and from every quarter the most thorough interpretation which is demanded by our times, and be shielded not only from every breath of error, but also from every temerarious opinion."[23]

Despite the stern tone of the letter, Leo emphasized three other significant aspects of the PBC's task:

1. "[N]one of the recent discoveries which the human mind has made are foreign to the purpose of their work."

2. Special attention is to be given to "the study of philology and kindred sciences," as well as to "the ancient and oriental languages."

3. The result of the PBC's work is described as "... furnishing to the Holy See an opportune occasion to declare what ought to be inviolably maintained by Catholics, what ought to be reserved for more profound research, and what ought to be left to the free judgment of each."

Each of these, coupled with the explicit pastoral concern that the explanation of the Scriptures offer "to the faithful a great source of spiritual profit," demonstrates Leo's balance with regard to modern biblical study. While the letter urged the PBC to determine *the* official meaning of certain texts, where that is obtainable, it also acknowledged that the church had not pronounced authoritative and restrictive interpretations of many biblical texts. In such instances, each expert would be free to hold whatever interpretation seemed best.

The establishment of the PBC gave the church a formal office to make pronouncements about biblical interpretation. Later, in 1904, the pope allowed the commission to grant ecclesiastical academic degrees. In time, it became one of the most prestigious centers in the world for higher biblical studies. From the perspective of scholarship, however, there were dark clouds on the horizon.

For decades under different popes, the PBC set about studying the biblical texts and issuing its findings. These were called *"responsa"* and were intended as responses to current questions being explored by scholars, often concerning the historicity of events recorded in the Bible. Under Pius X, Benedict XV, and Pius XI, the PBC scrutinized the work of Catholic biblical scholars with great care in order to forestall any possible aberration in their biblical scholarship. Numerous scholars fell under a cloud of suspicion. The PBC was especially concerned with the increasing historical skepticism that eminated from those employing modern scientific methods (historical criticism).

A particularly controversial period of the PBC's history lies between 1905 and 1915, to which we briefly drew attention in Part One. In the midst of the Modernist crisis, precipitated largely by the scholarly works of Alfred Loisy (using modern scientific methods of inquiry pioneered by Protestants), the Holy See became concerned about the erosion of doctrine in these new teachings. Consequently, the PBC issued a series of statements attempting to resolve definitively some controversial questions about the Bible, such as the Mosaic authorship of the Pentateuch, the basic historicity of the Bible, the historicity of the stories of creation in Genesis 1–3, the unity of the Book of Isaiah, the dating and authorship of the Gospels, Acts, and the Pauline letters, and so on. Although these statements contained much that was nuanced in response to complex questions, the tone was very conservative. The authoritative nature of the statements also dampened enthusiasm for the newer scientific methods of biblical studies. Catholic exegetes became fearful of censure for pursuing their studies, and several prominent scholars suffered as a result of the restrictive atmosphere.

Interestingly, the Holy See has never *officially* rescinded these early teachings of the PBC, despite the fact that contemporary scripture scholarship no longer holds most of the positions espoused by the commission. The reason is twofold. First, in 1955 Athanasius Miller and Arduin Kleinhans, the secretary and assistant secretary of the PBC at the time, issued a clarification of the early PBC teachings. The clarification indicated that Catholic scholars still had freedom to pursue their research on these matters provided that they did not impinge on questions of faith or morals and that they acknowledged the teaching role of the magisterium. A second reason was that, by the mid-1950s, there was general recognition that matters of authorship or dating of biblical books did not threaten the Catholic faith. Thus, Catholic scholars continue to debate such matters and weigh their convictions on the strength of their arguments, rather than on the authority of these early statements from the PBC. Indeed, later instructions of the PBC itself, especially the 1964 instruction on the historical truth of the Gospels, go well beyond these early instructions.

Throughout its history, the PBC has continued to issue documents on biblical topics, many of them quite important.[24] But in 1971, Pope Paul VI took a major step to reorganize the Roman curia and, in doing so, changed the status of the PBC. He made the PBC a consultative body of experts attached to the Congregation for the Doctrine of the Faith. As such, it comes under the direct authority of the prefect of that congregation and does not issue statements on its own authority. (The congregation has a comparable organ for investigating theological questions, the International Theological Commission, a body of expert theologians.) What does this shift mean for the PBC's authority?

Ultraconservatives have used the changed status of the PBC as an argument to dismiss any of the commission's teachings that they don't like. I think the situation is more complex. Cardinal Joseph Ratzinger, who went on to become Pope Benedict XVI, described the role of the "new" PBC when he promulgated its 1993 document, *The Interpretation of the Bible in the Church*, with these words:

> The Pontifical Biblical Commission, in its new form after the Second Vatican Council, is not an organ of the teaching office, but rather a commission of scholars who, in their scientific and ecclesial responsibility as believing exegetes, take positions on important problems of Scriptural interpretation and know that for this task *they enjoy the confidence of the teaching office*.[25]

The words I have emphasized are important. The commission's work, when accepted and promulgated by the congregation, expresses with some authority (limited though it may be) important Catholic positions. Ratzinger goes on to say,

[The document] contains a well-grounded overview of the panorama of present-day methods and in this way offers to the inquirer an orientation to the possibilities and limits of these approaches.... I hope that the document will have a wide circulation so that it becomes a genuine contribution to the search for a deeper assimilation of the word of God in Holy Scripture.[26]

These words offer strong endorsement of the general thrust of the PBC's document. I think it fair to say that it presents a proper Catholic approach to biblical interpretation today and cannot lightly be ignored.

Further support for this view is found in Pope John Paul II's address to the members of the PBC on April 23, 1993, on the occasion of accepting their document on interpretation. The pope's lengthy allocution affirmed several positive aspects of the PBC's instruction, especially its assertion that there is no "one" type of biblical interpretation that is Catholic. He said:

For Catholic exegesis does not have its own exclusive method of interpretation, but starting with the historico-critical basis freed from its philosophical presuppositions or those contrary to the truth of our faith, it makes the most of all current methods by seeking in each of them the "seeds of the Word."[27]

This acknowledgment of the foundational role of the historical-critical method, within a context of faith, is noteworthy. Much of the recent controversy about biblical studies has concerned this method. The pope went on to encourage the work of the commission with the following words:

Thanks to this document, the interpretation of the Bible in the Church will be able to obtain new vigor for the good of the whole world, so that the truth may shine forth and stir up charity on the threshold of the third millennium.... To this I add my warm encouragement for the next step to be taken. The increasing complexity of the task requires everyone's effort and a broad interdisciplinary cooperation. In a world where scientific research is taking on greater importance in many domains, it is indispensable for exegetical science to find its place at a comparable level.[28]

These words of encouragement to the PBC indicate the high esteem in which the Holy See holds the commission. It performs a vital service to the church, in the spirit of Vatican II, by providing expert guidance on technical matters that can directly impact how the church views the Scriptures today. The fact that both the pope and (then) Cardinal Ratzinger strongly confirmed the work of the PBC seems to indicate that the documents they produce are indeed a part of the church's compendium of authoritative teaching on the Bible. When promulgated with papal and dicasterial authority, these documents serve to guide Catholic scholars and laity on the arduous but rewarding path of biblical interpretation.

Despite its importance and its status as a dogmatic constitution, *Dei Verbum* is not the church's last word on Scripture. The magisterium continues to rely on the advice and expertise of the PBC to assist with important questions of biblical methodologies and interpretation that continue to arise. I will summarize several examples.

In 1984 the PBC issued a technical document in French and Latin titled "Scripture and Christology."[29] Its purpose was to offer assistance to "pastors and the faithful" about how to understand from the biblical perspective Jesus as messiah (the Christ). Joseph Fitzmyer, a principal commentator on the text, points to its twofold importance.[30] First, it emphasizes the need to consider the *total* biblical witness of the notion of the messiah. That is, one should not just rely on certain texts but review the whole of the biblical testimony. This is consistent with the teaching of *Dei Verbum* on a principle feature of Catholic interpretation (*DV*, 12; *CCC*, 112). Second, the document avoids any harmonization of the biblical data on Christology. Thus, there is no one Christology in the New Testament, but there are multiple "Christologies," or ways of understanding Jesus as the messiah. Unlike other PBC documents, this one was not issued with papal authority, yet it does serve as a reliable guide to a Catholic approach to this question.

We have already mentioned the 1993 PBC document, *The Interpretation of the Bible in the Church*. This text is important for several reasons. Issued under the authority of the Congregation for the Doctrine of the Faith and the approval of Pope John Paul II, the text reviews all the current major scholarly methods of biblical studies. It evaluates each method according to strengths and weaknesses, pointing out that no one method suffices for biblical study. Not only does the text insist that the historical-critical method remains "indispensable" (§I.A.1) but it also finds some value in virtually every approach to Scripture, including approaches from liberationist and feminist perspectives. In the end, the text affirms the direction set by *Dei Verbum*. Catholic interpretation employs both traditional approaches (e.g., patristic and spiritual forms of exegesis) and modern ones (e.g., historical-critical, sociological, and narrative-critical methods). The text explicitly affirms:

> Catholic exegesis does not claim any scientific method as its own. Consequently, Catholic exegesis freely makes use of the scientific methods and approaches which allow a better grasp of the meaning of texts in their linguistic, literary, socio-cultural, religious and historical contexts.... What characterizes Catholic exegesis is that it deliberately places itself within the living tradition of the Church, whose first concern is fidelity to the revelation attested by the Bible. (§III; cf. *DV*, 10 and 12).

In 2001 the PBC issued another important document that has both doctrinal and pastoral significance. Titled "The Jewish People and Their Sacred Scriptures in the Bible,"[31] it provides an extensive review of the biblical data on the image and representation of the Jewish people throughout the Old and New Testaments. Doctrinally, its importance is found in a sober and reasoned assessment of the role of Judaism in the founding of Christianity. Jesus was, of course, Jewish, and many of the early Christians (including Peter, Paul, etc.), were indeed Jews. Our Christian roots are deeply embedded within that Jewish heritage that impacted virtually every aspect of Christian life for centuries. Pastorally, the document provides a way of speaking about the Jews and seemingly anti-Jewish parts of the New Testament that at times have led to terrible anti-Semitic acts, such as the Holocaust (called by Jews the Shoah) during World War II. Pope John Paul II, who made relations with Jews a priority during his pontificate, approved this document and obviously was profoundly interested in it. It can be said to be in line with *Dei Verbum* in the sense that its method reflects the best of modern, scientific study of the Bible, and its pastoral application fulfills the constitution's encouragement of inter-faith dimensions of biblical studies (*DV*, 25; cf. *NA*, 4).

One can see from the quality of these PBC documents that the commission continues to offer useful and informative direction to the church on biblical issues of timely significance. If the nature of the commission's authority has changed, its ability to provide sound direction for magisterial teaching has not. The commission, in fact, is a distinctive aspect of the Catholic contribution to modern biblical studies of which Catholics can rightly be proud.

QUESTIONS OF TRANSLATION

One of the more controversial aspects of biblical studies after *Dei Verbum* concerns translation of the Bible. Two issues stand out: inclusive language and the authoritative status of the *Nova Vulgata* ("New Vulgate").

Inclusive Language

The controversy over inclusive language arose both in social and ecclesiastical contexts in the 1970s and 1980s. Stated briefly, the notion of inclusive language means language that should not offend people but provide an "inclusive" attitude toward all.[32] Some of the concern regarding this was promoted by feminists who believed that much biblical language was too "patriarchal" and "sexist," emphasizing only a male perspective. Other voices expressed concerns over inter-religious sensitivities (e.g., Jews find it offensive to speak the name of "God" directly), or over language that could be demeaning (e.g., the "blind," the "deaf" or the "crippled," seemingly overemphasizing the handicap rather than the person).

Another aspect of this controversy has to do with a limitation of the English language in comparison to other modern languages. In

English, "man" is a word that historically has done double duty. In the past, it meant both the male individual and humankind in general. In more modern usage, it has become more restricted to the former, and many find it improper to use it in its generic sense.

In essence, two schools of thought have arisen over this controversy. On the one side are those who believe that the task of translation must take into account changing meanings of words in any receptor language. Accurate translation involves more than simply rendering word-for-word and structure-for-structure the original language of an ancient text. It must also render the meanings of words and concepts not easily understood and easily misconstrued in the receptor language. On the other side are rightful concerns about bending to modern "political correctness," which at times gives undue emphasis to modern fads and ignores trustworthy ancient traditions.

The controversy intensified when certain translations of the Bible were issued that seemed "over the top" regarding the use of politically correct language. For example, one modern edition of the New Testament was quickly dubbed the "PC Bible" for some of its excesses, such as rendering the beginning of the Lord's Prayer with "Father-Mother."

Within the Catholic Church itself, examples of the controversy flourished. In 1994 the International Commission on English in the Liturgy (ICEL), a group of all the English-speaking bishops' conferences of the world, published a new edition of the psalms intended to be inclusive in its rendering. Roman authorities, however, later judged it to be much too free in its translation. Also, an ad hoc committee of the U.S. bishops themselves had produced a new translation of the psalms in 1991 for The New American Bible, in preparation for a revised lectionary. Although it was much more moderate in its proposed translation than the ICEL text and it received an imprimatur, ecclesiastical authorities did not allow it to be used for the revised lectionary because of some questions primarily directed toward its inclusive translation tendencies.

Yet another controversial topic was the translation of the *Catechism of the Catholic Church* (first edition, 1994).[33] Despite assurances from a rather conservative committee that its rendering of the Latin text was faithful to the original, Roman authorities deemed it to be too inclusive. When the translated text finally appeared, certain passages seemed unnecessarily to revert to exclusive or sexist language even where the original could allow a more inclusive translation.

One of the results of this unending debate was the entire reorganization of ICEL. Authorities in Rome were clearly displeased with ICEL's handling of many translation issues in recent years. The Congregation for Divine Worship and the Discipline of the Sacraments appointed a special committee of senior bishops from the English-speaking world (the *Vox Clara* Committee) to help oversee the work of translations. In addition, Rome guided the production of new statutes governing ICEL's work, and the commission was reorganized in 2003. These actions have shifted the weight of influence to more conservative voices who wish to control more tightly the process of liturgical and biblical translation.

Dei Verbum clearly sounded a call for new translations of the Bible that would promote accessibility to it (*DV*, 22). What it did not do was to give explicit guidelines on how best to accomplish this goal. Part of the agenda of the future will likely continue to be this issue of translation. If recent meetings of the USCCB are any indicator, these issues tend to bring out the serious underlying divisions over these issues, evident even among the bishops. Liturgical topics, in particular, induce an incredibly emotional reaction on the part of many of the bishops, even to the point of lengthy, tedious debates over minute points that some would say are hardly at the center of the faith.

The *Nova Vulgata*

A specific case in point over translation issues is the New Vulgate edition of the Bible. That the famous Latin Vulgate translation of the Bible done by St. Jerome in the fourth century AD retains a special revered status in Catholic history is undeniable. That it is supposed to transcend the Hebrew Bible (or Septuagint) and Greek New Testament as the authoritative source for biblical translations used in Catholic liturgy is another matter. This question was at the heart of a controversy that arose in 2001 when the Congregation for Divine Worship and the Discipline of the Sacraments issued an instruction, *Liturgiam Authenticam*. In order to understand why this document has caused concern among many biblical scholars, a little background is necessary.

Liturgiam Authenticam assigned a particularly authoritative role to the *Nova Vulgata* (1979), a new and definitive edition of the old Latin Vulgate (translated from the original biblical languages by St. Jerome). Pope Paul VI had requested such an updating of the Vulgate in 1965, partly because the Latin text was known to contain many errors that had accrued over time. His intention, which was never fully realized, was to produce a new Latin translation of the liturgy of the hours. He appointed a commission to accomplish the task, and Pope John Paul II promulgated the final text on April 25, 1979.

The Catholic Church has always expressed concern that the translations of the Bible used by Catholics be accurate and as faithful to the original text as possible (*DV*, 22). There will always be a need for new translations of the Bible for two primary reasons. First, our knowledge of the biblical languages, history, and background grows with each passing year. Sometimes important archaeological finds can shed light on the context of specific biblical references or help to explain obscure biblical customs. Second, since modern languages change with usage, there is a constant need to update expressions so that they communicate accurately the *meaning* of the text and not simply the *words*. In other words, literal translations do not *always* render faithfully the meaning of a text, whether because of limitations regarding how best to express a concept or because of the peculiarities of the receptor language. Biblical translation is sometimes as much art as it is science.

As we saw previously, Vatican II encouraged the production of modern (vernacular) translations of the Bible. *Dei Verbum* explicitly called for the production of ecumenical editions of the Bible with explanatory notes.

> Easy access to Sacred Scripture should be provided for all the Christian faithful. That is why the Church from the very beginning accepted as her own that very ancient Greek translation; of the Old Testament which is called the Septuagint; and she has always given a place of honor to other Eastern translations and Latin ones especially the Latin translation known as the Vulgate. But since the word of God should be accessible at all times, the Church by her authority and with

maternal concern sees to it that suitable and correct translations are made into different languages, especially from the original texts of the sacred books. And should the opportunity arise and the Church authorities approve, if these translations are produced in cooperation with the separated brethren as well, all Christians will be able to use them. (*DV*, 22)

Furthermore, editions of the Sacred Scriptures, provided with suitable footnotes, should be prepared also for the use of non-Christians and adapted to their situation. (*DV*, 25)

It comes as no surprise, then, that after Vatican II many translations of the Bible appeared. The most prominent Catholic translation in the United States was The New American Bible. As recommended by *Divino Afflante Spiritu* and *Dei Verbum*, experts made these translations from the original languages. So why the controversy over *Liturgiam Authenticam*?

The leadership of the Catholic Biblical Association of America, the most prestigious Catholic body of biblical scholars in the United States, wrote to the American bishops in 2001 explaining the difficulty of implementing the section of the document that attributes definitive authority to the *Nova Vulgata*. They specifically pointed to four problems.[34]

First, *Liturgiam Authenticam* proclaims the *Nova Vulgata* as the authoritative scriptural tradition in the church and requires that it be followed as the authoritative original text. The document bases its assertion on the alleged authority of St. Jerome's Vulgate, which, while it has been honored (along with the Septuagint) for its importance, has never been formally invested with inherent authority.

Second, ever since Pius XII's landmark encyclical *Divino Afflante Spiritu*, Catholic scholars have been encouraged to translate from the original biblical languages. Scholars regularly use the Vulgate (and the multiple Latin editions that were produced from it) primarily for comparative purposes, especially to help clarify obscure or particularly difficult passages. They suggested, therefore, that to use it as the basis for new liturgical translations flies in the face of this directive that was reinforced by Vatican II.

Third, when the *Nova Vulgata* finally appeared, the secretary of the PBC at the time noted explicitly that its purpose was to provide assistance for producing vernacular translations in instances where translators might not know the original Greek or Hebrew or when there were no other special resources that could be used. Thus, it seemingly was never meant to become the only edition from which liturgical translations should be done.

Finally, Catholic Biblical Association leaders note that the PBC was not consulted prior to the promulgation of *Liturgiam Authenticam*. Although the document concerns liturgy directly, its stepping into the area of biblical translations would seem to require that the church's official body of consultants on biblical matters should have been consulted.

On the other side of the controversy, of course, is the desire for uniformity in the liturgy. Many voices after the council bemoaned the fluidity of Roman Catholic liturgy. In comparison to the staid, unchanging Latin Mass of the pre–Vatican II church, modern liturgy in the vernacular exhibited much less uniformity around the world. Bible translations also varied, as several editions of the English Bible (i.e., The New American Bible with Revised New Testament [1986] and The Jerusalem Bible [1966]) were permitted for liturgical use for many years after Vatican II. These voices also desire that one biblical translation (such as the Revised Standard Version [1952]) be used for liturgies conducted in English. Opponents believe that *Liturgiam Authenticam* promotes a one-size-fits-all mentality that is not appropriate for the diversity of linguistic situations that exist in the English-speaking world.

At this writing, the Congregation for Divine Worship and the Discipline of the Sacraments is pushing forward the implementation of *Liturgiam Authenticam*. A new guiding document for translators of liturgical texts in English is under consideration. This draft document, titled *Ratio Translationis for the English Language* (2005), sets out translation principles based upon *Liturgiam Authenticam*; it will likely henceforth have an effect on the biblical texts used in liturgy.

I cannot say where this conversation will lead. All translators must reckon with *Liturgiam Authenticam*, which in itself contains many good instructions concerning the challenges of translations. But it looks as if controversies will continue in this area for some time to come.

ON popular level)

6. THE CHALLENGES OF BIBLICAL FUNDAMENTALISM

Without doubt, one of the greatest legacies of *Dei Verbum* has been the rediscovery of the Bible among Catholic laity. The combination of the liturgical reforms that flowed from Vatican II and the proliferation of publications, especially on the popular level, has led to greater interest in the Bible among Catholics than at any other time since the Protestant Reformation. Yet challenges abound in this arena.

The general impression in many quarters of the Catholic Church is that the increased interest in the Bible has not necessarily led to more knowledge. Many Catholics still feel uncomfortable among Protestant friends who, at least ostensibly, exhibit a greater knowledge of Bible facts or can quote favorite passages freely.

Many pastors complain that, despite expressed interest by parishioners in more adult education on the Bible, they do not always show up when such programs are offered. Then there is the proliferation of Bible study programs among many Protestant congregations that entice Catholics to participate. At times, these have good, knowledgeable leadership that can promote appropriate access to the Bible. Many times, however, such programs are promoted by aggressive fundamentalist groups interested in inserting a wedge between Catholics and their faith in order to lure them away, all under the mistaken notion that Catholicism does not promote authentic biblical faith.

Biblical fundamentalism is a particularly potent and influential force in the United States at the beginning of the twenty-first century. It is a complex phenomenon that has social and political, as well as religious, aspects to it.[35] The topic itself invites controversy. Most Catholic scholars believe that biblical fundamentalism goes against an authentic Catholic approach to the Bible. This position is reflected in *Dei Verbum* and in the Catechism, as we have pointed out in this book. The PBC also singled out fundamentalism as a virulent danger in its 1993 document, *The Interpretation of the Bible in the Church*. The commission said:

The fundamentalist approach is dangerous, for it is attractive to people who look to the Bible for ready answers to the problems of life. It can deceive these people, offering them interpretations that are pious but illusory, instead of telling them that the Bible does not contain an immediate answer to each and every problem. Without saying as much in so many words, fundamentalism actually invites people to a kind of intellectual suicide. It injects into life a false certitude, for it unwittingly confuses the divine substance of the biblical message with what are in fact its human limitations. (*IBC*, §I.F)

These are strong words. Some scholars have objected to this kind of warning and argued that it is an exaggeration that prevents more harmonious relations between Catholics and fundamentalists.[36] They believe that Catholic theologians and bishops have not delved into biblical fundamentalism with any real interest or depth, and the result has been an unbalanced caricature that does more harm than good. Others have pointed out that within Catholicism itself there exists a certain kind of fundamentalism, often associated with a naïve and rigid dogmatism that fails to account for the historical background of both the Bible and church teaching.[37]

One particularly public way in which biblical fundamentalism plays out even in the Catholic world is in the discussion of the theory of evolution. This famous debate, of course, reaches back into the early twentieth century and the infamous Scopes "monkey trial" in Tennessee. Ever since, biblical fundamentalists, among others, have sought to have the biblical understanding of creation, as expressed in Genesis 1–11, taught equally with the scientific theory of evolution. They have attempted various justifications for this, putting forth, most recently, the theory of "intelligent design." This theory asserts that haphazard evolution, based upon Charles Darwin's understanding of the survival of the fittest, cannot adequately explain the diversity or complexity of the universe as we know it. Nor does the theory of evolution properly take into account the uniqueness of human beings in the chain of life. Thus a higher, intelligent being must be behind evolution.

The debate has raged strongly, particularly in areas of the United States where public school curricula are at stake. Recently, the debate has heated up. The real question is now whether a biblical doctrine of creation (even in the more recent and sophisticated formulation of "intelligent design") should be taught side-by-side with a scientific theory.

Pope John Paul II pointed out in an address to the Pontifical Academy of Sciences in 1996 that a theory of evolution is not incompatible with Catholic faith. More startlingly, he suggested that it was more than a theory. Recent developments may indicate a shift in the Catholic position, however. In July 2005 Cardinal Christoph Schönborn, the archbishop of Vienna, entered the debate. He published an op-ed piece in the *New York Times* in which he suggested that the theory of Darwinian evolution is contrary to Catholic faith. He was quite dismissive of Pope John Paul II's earlier statement, saying that it was insignificant and not well developed. Essentially, he entered the debate in the United States over school curricula and allied himself with biblical fundamentalists trying to promote "creationism" as a viable and equally valid alternative to scientific theory. Overlooked in the debate is the fact that the kind of Darwinian theory of evolution targeted by such critics is actually not much in vogue in scientific circles these days. Theories of evolution have themselves evolved from the fairly primitive explanation promoted by Charles Darwin in the nineteenth century.

At the center of the controversy is the Bible itself as the highest authority, especially for those who are convinced that the early chapters of Genesis are to be taken literally. Most scholars who accept modern scientific study of the Bible look on this development with incredulity. In their view, the early chapters are clearly ancient Near Eastern mythology that embodies the truth that God is the true origin of the universe, but the story in all its details was never meant to be taken literally as scientific fact.

Some find a certain sense of déjà vu in this controversy. It recalls a much older one that set science in opposition to religion. Remember Galileo Galilei (1564–1642), who faced serious opposition to his scientific theory about the planets because of the contemporary understanding of the Bible? In one of his letters, he outlines wisely an approach that seems now, in hindsight, to be almost in the spirit of Vatican II (*DV*, 11):

> I believe that the intention of Holy Writ was to persuade men [sic] of the truths necessary for salvation, such as neither science nor any other means could render credible, but only the voice of the Holy Spirit. But I do not think it necessary to

believe that the same God who gave us our senses, our speech, our intellect, would have put aside the use of these, to teach us instead such things as with their help we could find out for ourselves, particularly in the case of these sciences of which there is not the smallest mention in the Scriptures; and above all, in astronomy, of which so little notice is taken that the names of none of the planets are mentioned. Surely, if the intention of the sacred scribes had been to teach people astronomy, they would not have passed over the subject so completely.[38]

Perhaps we are destined to revisit this battle time and again because how one views the Bible, specifically in its authority, its origins, and its purpose, is still crucial to current debates about religion and science. Given the ongoing influence of fundamentalists in American culture, such issues are not likely to die down any time soon. Catholics will have to reckon with biblical fundamentalism one way or another. We cannot ignore the contemporary challenges to biblical interpretation that find their way even into daily life.

CONCLUSION

These six points do not constitute the limit of current controversies and discussions about biblical interpretation that have emerged in the church's discourse since *Dei Verbum*. They are, however, important barometers of such discussions that will surely continue indefinitely into the future. If *Dei Verbum* did not resolve all the issues surrounding the Bible and its role in the church's life, it certainly gave them a powerful boost. Thanks to this remarkable constitution, and the visionary council fathers who produced it, the landscape of the church has changed forever.

We would not exaggerate to claim that *Dei Verbum* fostered a peaceful revolution. Scripture has once more become the "soul of sacred theology" (*DV*, 24) and there can be no turning back from the path that the constitution has laid out for the future. Wisely, the constitution left some issues unresolved precisely because the times were not yet right for their definitive resolution. That is why debates, discussions, dialogues, and even controversies will continue as the entire church seeks to reflect on this precious gift God has given us "for the sake of our salvation." As the constitution itself so beautifully says in the first paragraph that begins the last chapter:

> For in the sacred books, the Father who is in heaven meets his children with great love and speaks with them; and the force and power in the Word of God is so great that it stands as the support and energy of the Church, the strength of faith for her sons, the food of the soul, the pure and everlasting source of spiritual life. (*DV*, 21)

NOTES

PREFACE

1. Quoted online through *Zenit*, October 11, 2005 (ZE05101104), http://www.zenit.org. Levada made his remarks during a lecture titled *"Dei Verbum*—quarant' anni dopo," at the Pontificio Ateneo Sant'Anselmo in Rome on October 10, 2005, to commemorate the constitution's fortieth anniversary.

PART I: THE DOCUMENT

1. For more details see, Andrea Riccardi, "The Tumultuous Opening Days of the Council," in Alberigo, *Vatican II*, 2:11.

2. Quoted in Yves Congar, *Report from Rome: On the First Session of the Vatican Council*, trans. A. Manson (Liverpool: Geoffrey Chapman, 1963), 101–2.

3. This point itself has become the subject of debate. Some think that Vatican II was as doctrinal as any other council. Conversely, some point out that Vatican Council I was much more pastoral than is usually assumed. The debate itself will likely continue. For diverse assessments, see Edward T. Oakes, "Was Vatican II a Liberal or Conservative Council?" *ChicSt* 43:2 (2004): 191–211; Joseph A. Komonchak, "Is Christ Divided? Dealing with Diversity and Disagreement," *Origins* 33:9 (July 17, 2003): 140–48; and John W. O'Malley, "One Priesthood: Two Traditions," in *A Concert of Charisms: Ordained Ministry in Religious Life*, ed. Paul K. Hennesy (New York/Mahwah, NJ: Paulist Press, 1997), 9–24, esp. p. 15.

4. See Hilari Raguer, "An Initial Profile of the Assembly," in Alberigo, *Vatican II*, 2:168, n. 4.

5. Vatican II's sixteen documents (also called generically "decrees") fall into three formal categories, constitutions, declarations, and decrees. The four constitutions (*SC*, *LG*, *DV*, and *GS*) have the highest authority, followed by the declarations and then the decrees. This distinction about the level of authority makes no presumptions on the influence that any of the individual

documents has exercised in the life of the church. Each decree in its own way has significantly impacted the church's life.

6. For an overview, see Alexa Suelzer and John S. Kselman, "Modern Old Testament Criticism," and John S. Kselman and Ronald D. Witherup, "New Testament Criticism," *NJBC*, §69 and §70, respectively.

7. The history of the English Bible provides fascinating reading. For a brief overview, see Raymond E. Brown, D. W. Johnson, and Kevin G. O'Connell, "Texts and Versions," *NJBC*, §68:189–216.

8. See Stanislas Lyonnet, "A Word on Chapters IV and VI of *Dei Verbum*," in René Latourelle, ed., *Vatican II: Assessment and Perspectives Twenty-Five Years After (1962–1987)*, 3 vols. (New York/Mahwah, NJ: Paulist Press, 1988–1989), 1:187. In 1816 Pope Pius VII censured a bishop for recommending that laity read the Bible!

9. Enzo Bianchi, "The Centrality of the Word of God," in *The Reception of Vatican II*, ed. Giuseppe Alberigo, Jean Pierre Jossua, and Joseph A. Komonchak (Washington, DC: Catholic University Press, 1987), 115, emphasis in the original.

10. For more on this topic, see Keith Clements, "*Sola scriptura*," in *A New Dictionary of Christian Theology*, ed. Alan Richardson and John Bowden (London: SCM, 1983), 546.

11. See Gerald P. Fogarty, *American Catholic Biblical Scholarship: A History from the Early Republic to Vatican II* (San Francisco: Harper & Row, 1989), 322, who refers to the work of Hubert Jedin, the famed scholar of the Council of Trent.

12. It is worth noting that Protestantism had its own struggles with scientific methods of biblical studies. In the 1890s, for instance, Charles Augustus Briggs (1841–1913), a professor and vigorous proponent of historical criticism at Union Theological Seminary in New York, was tried in the Presbyterian Church for heresy. For more on this trial, see Fogarty, *American Catholic Biblical Scholarship*, 140–70.

13. Interestingly, the Dominican Marie-Joseph Lagrange (1855–1938), one of the great modern Catholic biblical pioneers and founder of the École Biblique in Jerusalem, who died prior to the publication of Pius XII's encyclical, considered Leo XIII's encyclical to be the Magna Carta of Catholic biblical studies. This hints at how forward-thinking Leo's encyclical actually was.

14. In particular, see the volumes of Alberigo, *Vatican II*, listed in Further Reading.

15. In Vorgrimler, *Commentary*, 3:159.

16. Ibid., 323–25.

17. See Barnabas Ahern, "Scriptural Aspects," in *Vatican II: An Interfaith Appraisal,* ed. John H. Miller (Notre Dame: University of Notre Dame, 1966), 66, n. 8.

18. Joseph Ratzinger, *Theological Highlights of Vatican II* (New York/ Mahwah, NJ: Paulist Press, 1966), 20–21.

19. See Robert E. Tracy, *American Bishop at the Vatican Council* (New York: McGraw-Hill, 1966), 77; also Xavier Rynne, *Vatican Council II* (Mary-knoll, NY: Orbis, 1999), 89–90.

20. Thus, Giuseppe Ruggieri, "The First Doctrinal Clash," in Alberigo, *Vatican II,* 2:264.

21. Fogarty, *American Catholic Biblical Scholarship,* 332–33.

22. See Hanjo Sauer, "The Doctrinal and the Pastoral: The Text on Divine Revelation," in Alberigo, *Vatican II,* 4:210–31, from which this information is summarized.

23. Quoted in *Third Session Council Speeches of Vatican II,* ed. William K. Leahy and Anthony T. Massimini (Glen Rock, NJ: Paulist Press, 1966), 79.

24. See Leahy and Massimini, *Third Session,* 85.

25. Ibid., 87–90.

26. See Sauer, "Doctrinal and Pastoral," in Alberigo, *Vatican II,* 4:223, and Thomas McGovern, "The Interpretation of Scripture 'in the Spirit': The Edelby Intervention at Vatican II," *ITQ* 64:3 (1999): 245–59. The text of Edelby's intervention is most accessible in Gerald O'Collins's *Retrieving Fundamental Theology: The Three Styles of Contemporary Theology* (New York/Mahwah, NJ: Paulist Press, 1993), Appendix 1, 174–77.

27. From an Eastern rite standpoint, *Dei Verbum*'s strong christological orientation tends to minimize both the trinitarian dimension of revelation and the role of the Holy Spirit, although some would view this more as a question of emphasis than of substance.

28. See the assessment of O'Collins, *Retrieving Fundamental Theology,* 56.

29. See Leahy and Massimini, *Third Session,* 94–97.

30. Ibid., 90–94. We should keep in mind that many interventions were not done orally in the aula but by means of written responses. One bishop whose written recommendations scholars believe impacted the highly christological orientation of the constitution was Bishop Paul-Joseph Schmitt of Metz (France). See Carmen Aparicio, "Bishop Paul-Joseph Schmitt and Vatican II: Jesus Christ, the Fullness of Revelation," in *The Convergence of Theology: Festschrift for Gerald O'Collins,* ed. Daniel Kendall and Stephen T. Davis (New York/Mahwah, NJ: Paulist Press, 2001), 87–108.

31. See Alberigo, *Vatican II,* 4:226.

32. Quoted in *American Participation in the Second Vatican Council*, ed. Vincent A. Yzermans (New York: Sheed and Ward, 1967), 96–97. For a fuller treatment of Neuner's views, see Sauer, "Doctrinal and Pastoral," in Alberigo, *Vatican II*, 4:201–2.

33. Thus, Rino Fisichella and René Latourelle, "Dei Verbum," in their *Dictionary of Fundamental Theology*, Eng. ed. R. Latourelle (New York: Crossroad, 1994), 217. Cardinal Ermenegildo Florit (Florence) was instrumental in keeping the document on track.

34. For details, see Ratzinger, "Chapter Two," in Vorgrimler, *Commentary*, 2:194–95.

35. Joseph Ratzinger, "Preface," in Vorgrimler, *Commentary*, 3:167.

36. Fogarty, *American Catholic Biblical Scholarship*, 343.

37. See Vorgrimler, *Commentary*, 3:165–66.

38. Ibid., 3:184.

39. See Yves M.-J. Congar, *Tradition and Traditions: The Biblical, Historical, and Theological Evidence for Catholic Teaching on Tradition* (San Diego: Basilica Press; New York: Simon & Schuster, 1966; French originals 1960 and 1963); and *The Meaning of Tradition* (New York: Hawthorn Books, 1964; French original 1963).

40. See Herbert Vorgrimler, "Karl Rahner: The Theologian's Contribution," in *Vatican II Revisited by Those Who Were There*, ed. Alberic Stacpoole (Minneapolis: Winston Press, 1986), 32–46.

PART II: MAJOR POINTS

1. This connects with the affirmation in *Nostra Aetate*, the Declaration on the Relation of the Church to Non-Christian Religions, that the Jews mediated and preserved these sacred writings (*NA*, 4).

2. See Joseph Fitzmyer's comments in *Vatican II: Forty Personal Stories*, ed. William Madges and Michael J. Daley (Mystic, CT: Twenty-Third Publications, 2003), 136; also José Caba, "Historicity of the Gospels (*Dei Verbum* 19): Genesis and Fruits of the Conciliar Text," in René Latourelle, ed., *Vatican II: Assessment and Perspectives Twenty-Five Years After (1962–1987)*, 3 vols. (New York/Mahwah, NJ: Paulist Press, 1988–1989), 1:299–320.

3. The official observer was Max Thurian, a monk from the famous interfaith community of Taizé, France. See Latourelle, *Vatican II*, 1:175.

4. The exact line is, "He is present in His word, since it is He Himself who speaks when the holy scriptures are read in the Church." This is one of several "presences" of Christ in the church's liturgy outlined in *SC*, i.e., in the eucharistic species, in the person of the minister, in the sacraments, and in the assembly gathered for worship.

5. See especially Stanislas Lyonnet, "A Word on Chapters IV and VI of *Dei Verbum*," in Latourelle, *Vatican II*, 1:157–207, who makes several of the points that follow.

6. This is the judgment of S. Lyonnet, ibid., 188. One should note that Leo XIII's approach expressed in *Providentissimus Deus* (article 15) was virtually anti-ecumenical and condescending toward non-Catholic interpretation of Scripture.

7. Vorgrimler, *Commentary*, 3:164–65. Ratzinger also notes that the minority was not satisfied with the final schema submitted for vote on October 29, 1965, and circulated a pamphlet to that effect, but it exercised no influence on the outcome.

8. This translation does not adequately reflect the Latin text. A better translation is found in Norman Tanner, ed., *Decrees of the Ecumenical Councils*, 2 vols. (London: Sheed & Ward, subsequently Continuum/Washington, DC: Georgetown University Press, 1990), 2:976: "...we must acknowledge that the books of scripture teach firmly, faithfully, and without error such truth as God, for the sake of our salvation, wished the biblical text to contain."

9. H. Sauer, "The Doctrinal and the Pastoral," in Alberigo, *Vatican II*, 4:220. Cardinal Bea comments that "a long and wearisome debate" preceded this resolution. Bea, *Word*, 188.

10. Barnabas Ahern, "Scriptural Aspects," in *Vatican II: An Interfaith Appraisal*, ed. John H. Miller (Notre Dame: University of Notre Dame, 1966), 58, 66; also Christopher Butler, *The Theology of Vatican II*, rev. ed. (Westminster, Maryland: Christian Classics, 1981; orig. 1967), 49, 51.

11. In Vorgrimler, *Commentary*, 3:184–90.

12. A helpful survey of theories of inspiration is found in Raymond F. Collins, "Inspiration," *NJBC*, §65.

13. Ahern, "Scriptural Aspects," in Miller, *Vatican II*, 65.

PART III: IMPLEMENTATION

1. Edward Schillebeeckx, *The Real Achievement of Vatican II* (New York: Herder and Herder, 1967), 39.

2. Ibid.

3. Ibid., 40–41.

4. Avery Dulles, *Revelation and the Quest for Unity* (Washington, DC: Corpus Books, 1968), 82–99.

5. Ibid., 90.

6. Ibid., 91.

7. Ibid., 93.

8. Carroll Stuhlmueller, "Vatican II and Biblical Criticism," in *The Impact of Vatican II*, ed. John Ford, et al. (St. Louis: B. Herder, 1966), 27–43.

9. See Senior, "Dogmatic Constitution on Divine Revelation," in *Vatican II and Its Documents: An Appraisal*, ed. Timothy E. O'Connell, Theology and Life Series 15 (Wilmington, DE: Michael Glazier, 1986), 122–40.

10. Ibid., 138–39.

11. Jerome H. Neyrey, "Interpretation of Scripture in the Life of the Church," in *Vatican II: The Unfinished Agenda*, ed. Lucien Richard, et al. (Wilmington, DE: Michael Glazier, 1987), 33–46.

12. See the multiple entries in Further Reading.

13. John R. Donahue, "The Bible and Catholic Social Teaching: Will This Engagement Lead to Marriage?" in *Modern Catholic Social Teaching: Commentaries and Interpretations*, ed. Kenneth R. Himes (Washington: Georgetown University, 2005), 9–40.

14. See Hanjo Sauer, "The Doctrinal and the Pastoral: The Text on Divine Revelation," in Alberigo, *Vatican II*, 4:208.

15. Paul S. Minear, "A Protestant Point of View," in *Vatican II: An Interfaith Appraisal*, ed. John H. Miller (Notre Dame: University of Notre Dame, 1966), 68–88.

16. The word "dogmatic" appears in the final published edition of *Dei Verbum* but for unknown reasons was left off a draft of the schema. See H. Sauer, "The Doctrinal and Pastoral Text," in Alberigo, *Vatican II*, 4:197.

17. See Robert E. Carbonneau, "The Genesis of *The Bible Today*," *BibToday* 40:5 (2002): 273–77.

18. John Paul II, *Theology of the Body: Human Love in the Divine Plan* (Boston: Pauline Books and Media, 1998).

19. See J. Michael Miller, ed., *Encyclicals* in Further Reading; also J. Michael Miller, "Interior Intelligibility: The Use of Scripture in Papal and Conciliar Documents," *Canadian Catholic Review* 11 (Sept. 1993): 9–18; and Terrence Prendergast, "A Vision of Wholeness: A Reflection on the Use of Scripture in a Cross-Section of Papal Writings," in *The Thought of John Paul II*, ed. John M. McDermott (Rome: Gregorian University Press, 1993), 81.

20. For an overview of the Catechism's teaching on Scripture, see Thomas McGovern, "The New Catechism and Scripture," *HomPastRev* (1996): 8–16.

21. Private audience, CBF Executive Committee, April 7, 1986; quoted on CBF website, www.c-b-f.org/start.php?CONTID=01_02_00&LANG=e.

22. Raymond E. Brown, Karl P. Donfried, and John Reumann, eds., *Peter in the New Testament* (Minneapolis: Augsburg; New York: Paulist Press, 1973).

23. Raymond E. Brown, Karl P. Donfried, Joseph A. Fitzmyer, and John Reumann, eds., *Mary in the New Testament* (Philadelphia: Fortress; New York/Mahwah, NJ: Paulist Press, 1978).

24. John Reumann, *Righteousness in the New Testament* (Philadelphia: Fortress; New York/Mahwah, NJ: Paulist Press, 1982).

25. See "Report on Sacred Scripture," *Origins* 29:17 (1999): 266–68.

26. Michael J. Gorman, ed., *An Ecumenical Introduction to the Bible and Its Interpretation* (Peabody, MA: Hendrickson, 2005).

27. See Walter Kasper, *Jesus the Christ*, trans. V. Green (London: Burns and Oates; New York: Paulist Press, 1976); Edward Schillebeeckx, *Jesus: An Experiment in Christology*, trans. Hubert Hoskins (New York: Seabury, 1979); and *Christ: The Experience of Jesus as Lord*, trans. John Bowden (New York: Seabury, 1980).

28. In addition to Brown's books listed in Further Reading, see his articles, "The Meaning of the Bible," *TD* 28:4 (1980): 305–20, and "'And the Lord said'? Biblical Reflections on Scripture as the Word of God," *TS* 42 (1981): 3–19.

29. See the exposition of Avery Dulles, "The Reception of Vatican II at the Extraordinary Synod of 1985," in *The Reception of Vatican II*, ed. Giuseppe Alberigo, Jean Pierre Jossua, and Joseph A. Komonchak (Washington, DC: Catholic University Press, 1987), 349–63.

30. For a critical review, see Mark Allan Powell, *Jesus as a Figure in History* (Louisville: Westminster John Knox, 1998), 65–81.

31. See Richard J. Neuhaus, ed., *Biblical Interpretation in Crisis: The Ratzinger Conference on Bible and Church*, Encounter Series 9 (Grand Rapids: Eerdmans, 1989), 5.

32. Quoted in *Origins* 17:35 (February 11, 1988): 595. Brown himself was a speaker at the same symposium where Ratzinger made his comments, and his talk defended properly exercised historical criticism. See Neuhaus, *Biblical Interpretation*, 24–49.

33. See articles by Maria Gapinski and Sal Ciresi in *The Arlington Catholic Herald* (June 26 and July 7, 2003). The fact that a diocesan newspaper carried this information and reported it as if it were solid Catholic teaching is most unfortunate.

34. English text from "On 'Dei Verbum' and Reading Scripture," www.zenit.org (November 11, 2005), ZE05110601.

PART IV: THE STATE OF THE QUESTIONS

1. For an overview, see Raymond F. Collins, "Inspiration," *NJBC*, §65; Richard Gaillardetz, *By What Authority? A Primer on Scripture, the Magisterium, and the Sense of the Faithful* (Collegeville: Liturgical Press, 2003), 15–40; and Paul J. Achtemeier, *Inspiration and Authority: Nature and Function of Christian Scripture* (Peabody, MA: Hendrickson, 1999).

2. Bea, *Word*, 187.

3. Ibid., 143.

4. Ibid., 147.

5. Ibid., 148.

6. For a summary of this process, see Raymond E. Brown and Raymond F. Collins, "Canonicity," *NJBC*, §66.

7. Bea, *Word*, 158.

8. Expressed in *Vatican II: An Interfaith Appraisal*, ed. John H. Miller (Notre Dame, IN: University of Notre Dame, 1966), 89. Butler was quick to point out, however, that he considered *Dei Verbum* "a milestone on an uncompleted journey." Ibid., 52. For him, the conversation over the nature of Tradition still required ongoing exploration.

9. John R. Donahue, "Between Jerusalem and Athens," in *Hermes and Athena: Biblical Exegesis and Philosophical Theology*, ed. Eleonore Stump and Thomas P. Flint (Notre Dame, IN: University of Notre Dame, 1993), 291.

10. Good overviews upon which some of this section is based are found in Joseph A. Fitzmyer, "Historical Criticism: Its Role in Biblical Interpretation and Church Life," *TS* 50 (1989): 244–59, and Raymond E. Brown, "The Contribution of Historical Biblical Criticism to Ecumenical Church Discussion," in *Biblical Interpretation in Crisis: The Ratzinger Conference on the Bible and Church*, ed. Richard John Neuhaus, Encounter Series 9 (Grand Rapids: Eerdmans, 1989), 24–49.

11. For an example of this and other criticisms, see Ignace de la Potterie, "Interpretation of Holy Scripture in the Spirit in Which It Was Written (*Dei Verbum* 12c)," in René Latourelle, ed., *Vatican II: Assessment and Perspectives Twenty-Five Years After (1962–1987)*, 3 vols. (New York/Mahwah, NJ: Paulist Press, 1988–1989), 1:220–66.

12. One example is the ecumenical "Ancient Christian Commentary on Scripture" series published by InterVarsity Press. These commentaries on each book of the Bible assemble excerpts on Scripture from Patristic commentaries and other early writings from the end of the New Testament era to around AD 750. An example of emphasis on the spiritual message of Scripture is the series of Spiritual Commentaries published by New City Press.

13. Marion L. Soards, "Appendix IX: The Question of a PreMarcan Passion Narrative?" in *The Death of the Messiah*, vol. 2, Raymond E. Brown (ABRL; New York: Doubleday, 1994), 1492–1524.

14. See especially Joseph A. Fitzmyer, "Raymond E. Brown, S.S.: In Memoriam," *USQR* 52 (1998): 1–18.

15. Quoted in Vorgrimler, *Commentary*, 3:158. Ratzinger later had reservations about the excesses of the historical-critical method, as expressed in his New York address, "Biblical Interpretation in Crisis: On the Question

of the Foundations and Approaches of Exegesis Today," in *Biblical Interpretation in Crisis*, ed. R. Neuhaus, 1–23. I would emphasize, however, that Ratzinger's complaints are directed more toward a type of historical-critical methodology characterized by the work of Rudolph Bultmann and Martin Dibelius that is not current today. He even admits, "The methods are often applied with a good deal of prudence, and the radical hermeneutics of the kind I have just described have already been disavowed by a large number of exegetes." Ibid., 5.

16. Useful surveys are found in John R. Donahue, "Modern and Post Modern Critical Methods of Biblical Study," in *Scripture: An Ecumenical Introduction to the Bible and Its Interpretation*, ed. Michael Gorman (Peabody, MA: Hendrickson, 2005), 147–62; Raymond E. Brown and Sandra Schneiders, "Hermeneutics," *NJBC*, §71; and Terence J. Keegan, *Interpreting the Bible: A Popular Introduction to Biblical Hermeneutics* (New York/Mahwah, NJ: Paulist Press, 1985).

17. Interestingly, the PBC issued the document under the authority of Pope John Paul II and Cardinal Ratzinger. The fact that the commission even acknowledged contributions of both feminist and liberationist interpretations is important, for Cardinal Ratzinger had earlier explicitly mentioned these two practices in a negative fashion. See Ratzinger, "Biblical Interpretation in Crisis," in *Biblical Interpretation in Crisis*, ed. R. Neuhaus, 5.

18. Later expanded and published in Luke Timothy Johnson and William S. Kurz, *The Future of Catholic Biblical Scholarship: A Constructive Conversation* (Grand Rapids: Eerdmans, 2002), 3–63.

19. Roland E. Murphy, "What Is Catholic About Catholic Biblical Scholarship—Revisited?" *BTB* 28 (1998): 112–19.

20. Peter S. Williamson, *Catholic Principles for Interpreting Scripture: A Study of the Pontifical Biblical Commission's* The Interpretation of the Bible in the Church, Subsidia biblica 22 (Rome: Pontifical Biblical Institute, 2001), digested in his "Catholic Principles for Interpreting Scripture," *CBQ* 65 (2003): 327–49. Williamson tries as much as possible to retain the language of the PBC document; I have shortened many of his descriptions, for the sake of space and succinctness.

21. See his essays in Johnson and Kurz, *The Future of Catholic Biblical Scholarship*, 159–248.

22. See Lewis Ayres and Stephen Fowl, "(Mis)Reading the Face of God: The Interpretation of the Bible in the Church," *TS* 60:3 (1999): 513–28, and the strong response by the late Roland E. Murphy, "Is the Paschal Mystery Really the Primary Hermeneutical Principle?" *TS* 61:1 (2000): 139–46.

23. Quoted in James J. McGivern's *Bible Interpretation* (Wilmington, NC: McGrath, 1978), 222.

24. A helpful summary of many of these documents can be found in Raymond E. Brown and Thomas Aquinas Collins, "Church Pronouncements," in *NJBC*, 72:25–39.

25. See *The Interpretation of the Bible in the Church* (Boston: St. Paul Books and Media, 1993), 28 (emphasis added by the author). This edition contains both the preface by Cardinal Ratzinger and the address to the commission by John Paul II when he received their document.

26. Ibid., 28–29.

27. Ibid., 23.

28. Ibid., 24–25.

29. See Joseph A. Fitzmyer, *Scripture and Christology: A Statement of the Biblical Commission with a Commentary* (New York/Mahwah, NJ: Paulist Press, 1986). According to Fitzmyer, who offers an "unofficial" English translation, the Latin text is the authoritative one, although the French text is at times clearer and was the working text of the PBC.

30. Ibid., 55–56.

31. See *The Jewish People and Their Sacred Scriptures in the Bible* (Boston: Pauline Books & Media, 2002).

32. For more detailed information, see Ronald D. Witherup, *A Liturgist's Guide to Inclusive Language* (Collegeville: Liturgical Press, 1996).

33. See Douglas Kent Clark, "On 'Englishing' the Catechism," *Living Light* 29 (1993): 13–28, and William J. Levada, "The Problem with 'Englishing' the Catechism," *Living Light* 30 (1994): 18–25.

34. See Joseph Jensen's summary of the issues in *"Liturgiam Authenticam* and the New Vulgate," *America* 185:4 (August 13–20, 2001): 11–13. For a detailed analysis, see Peter Jeffery, *Translating Tradition: A Chant Historian Reads* Liturgiam Authenticam (Collegeville: Liturgical Press, 2005).

35. For an overview and more resources, see Ronald D. Witherup, *Biblical Fundamentalism: What Every Catholic Should Know* (Collegeville: Liturgical Press, 2001).

36. For example, William M. Shea, "Fundamentalism: How Catholics Approach It," in *Christianity and the Stranger: Historical Essays*, ed. Francis W. Nichols (Atlanta: Scholars Press, 1995), 221–86, and his essay, "Catholic Reaction to Fundamentalism," *TS* 57 (1996): 264–86.

37. For example, Peter Henrici, "Is There Such a Thing as Catholic Fundamentalism?" *Communio* 28 (2001): 599–609, and Patrick M. Arnold, "The Rise of Catholic Fundamentalism," *America* 156 (1987): 297–302.

38. Quoted in Dana Sobel's *Galileo's Daughter: A Historical Memoir of Science, Faith, and Love* (New York: Walker, 1999), 65.

PART V
FURTHER READING

THE STORY AT VATICAN II

Alberigo, Giuseppe and Joseph A. Komonchak, eds. *History of Vatican II*. Maryknoll, NY: Orbis/Leuven: Peeters, 1995–2005. 5 vols. The most comprehensive history of the council, with extensive comments on many other aspects of the documents. For specific extensive treatment of *Dei Verbum*, see vol. 1, 167–356; vol. 2, 233–66, 385–91; vol. 4, 195–231; vol. 5, 275–362.

Congar, Yves. *Report from Rome: On the First Session of the Vatican Council*. Trans. A. Manson. Liverpool: Geoffrey Chapman, 1963, esp. pp. 57–65. A personal and insightful analysis by one of the most influential theologians behind the council.

———. *Mon journal du concile*, 2 vols. Paris: Cerf, 2000. The extensive diary of the author's experiences and observations at the council.

Fesquet, Henri. *The Drama of Vatican II: The Ecumenical Council, June, 1962–December, 1965*. Trans. Bernard Murchland. New York: Random House, 1967. A convenient digest of all four sessions of the council, focusing on the proceedings and interventions, as well as comments from and interviews with both participants and observers.

Grootaers, Jan. *Actes et Acteurs à Vatican II*. BETL 139. Leuven: Leuven University, 1998. A unique collection of essays on significant figures at the council, such as John XXIII, Cardinals Montini, Wojtyla, Bea, Suenens, Willebrands, and Alfrink.

Latourelle, René, ed. *Vatican II: Assessment and Perspectives Twenty-Five Years After (1962–1987)*, 3 vols. New York/Mahwah, NJ: Paulist Press, 1988–1989. An excellent compendium of essays on the history and interpretation of the council. On *Dei Verbum*, see especially vol. 1, 157–207, 220–66, 299–320.

143

Leahy, William K. and Anthony T. Massimini, eds. *Third Session Council Speeches of Vatican II*. Glen Rock, NJ: Paulist Press, 1966. A collection of some of the important speeches at the third session of the council. On *Dei Verbum*, see pp. 79–97.

Madges, William and Michael J. Daley, eds. *Vatican II: Forty Personal Stories*. Mystic, CT: Twenty-Third Publications, 2003. Interesting personal perspectives on Vatican II from a wide variety of individuals.

McAfee Brown, Robert. *Observer in Rome: A Protestant Report on the Vatican Council*. Garden City, NY: Doubleday, 1964. A perceptive analysis by a well-known Protestant observer at the council.

Pratt, James Francis Xavier. *The Day Neo-Scholasticism Died: November 20, 1962*. Ph.D. Diss.; Vanderbilt University, 2002. An unpublished but important dissertation that thoroughly examines the process of drafting *Dei Verbum*, indicating a dramatic shift in theological perspective at Vatican II.

Ruggieri, Giuseppe. "The First Doctrinal Clash." In *History of Vatican II*, ed. Giuseppe Alberigo and Joseph A. Komonchak, vol. 2, 233–66. Maryknoll, NY: Orbis, 1997. A good narrative recounting of the first ideological clashes at the council.

Rynne, Xavier. *Letters from Vatican City*, 4 vols. New York: Faber and Faber, 1963–1966. Reprint Maryknoll, NY: Orbis, 1999. Lively and pseudonymously published accounts of discussions and events at each session of the council by a journalist covering it, who later admitted to being Redemptorist Father Francis Xavier Murphy.

Sullivan, Maureen. *101 Questions and Answers on Vatican II*. New York/Mahwah, NJ: Paulist Press, 2002. A short introduction to the council in the well-known question-and-answer format.

Théobald, Christophe. "The Church Under the Word of God." In *History of Vatican II*, ed. Giuseppe Alberigo and Joseph A. Komonchak, vol. 5, 275–362. Maryknoll, NY: Orbis, 2005. An extensive and detailed account of the discussions leading up to the final edition of *Dei Verbum* at the last session of the council.

Tracy, Robert E. *American Bishop at the Vatican Council*. New York: McGraw-Hill, 1966. An interesting memoir by the bishop of Baton Rouge about his personal experience of the council.

Yzermans, Vincent A., ed. *American Participation in the Second Vatican Council*. New York: Sheed and Ward, 1967. Excellent essays summarizing the main contributions of American bishops and theologians at the council.

TEXTS, COMMENTARIES, AND DICTIONARIES

Abbott, Walter M., ed. *The Documents of Vatican II*. New York: America Press, 1966 and reprints. The first English translations of the council documents, some of which were rather hastily done but are nevertheless good translations.

Anderson, Floyd, ed. *Council Daybook*, 3 vols. Washington, DC: National Catholic Welfare Conference, 1965–1966. An extensive collection of speeches and interventions at all four sessions of the council.

✓ Bea, Augustin. *The Word of God and Mankind*. Chicago: Franciscan Herald Press, 1967. An extensive commentary on *Dei Verbum* by one of its influential framers.

Béchard, Dean P., ed. and trans. *The Scripture Documents: An Anthology of Official Catholic Teachings*. Collegeville: Liturgical Press, 2002. A recent collection of excerpts from the major teachings of the Roman Catholic Church on Scripture, covering councils from Trent to Vatican II, papal pronouncements, and curial documents.

Burrigana, Riccardo. *La Bibbia nel concilio: La redazione della costituzione "Dei Verbum" del Vaticano II*. Bologna: Società Editrice Il Mulino, 1998. An extensive study of the history of *Dei Verbum*; not yet translated into English but utilized in the Alberigo/Komonchak volumes above.

Butler, Christopher. *The Theology of Vatican II*, rev. ed. Westminster, Maryland: Christian Classics, 1981; orig. 1967. Essentially a commentary on the documents of Vatican II from one who was a participant and significant theological adviser during the last two years of the council; comments on *Dei Verbum* on pp. 25–51.

Catechism of the Catholic Church. 2d ed. Vatican City: Libreria Editrice Vaticana, 1997. The basic resource for Catholic teaching today.

Fisichella, Rino and René Latourelle. "Dei Verbum." In *Dictionary of Fundamental Theology*, ed. R. Latourelle and R. Fisichella; Eng. ed. R. Latourelle, 214–24. New York: Crossroad, 1994. A brief but helpful survey of basic information on *Dei Verbum*. The dictionary also contains many helpful definitions of theological terms that relate to the document.

Flannery, Austin, gen. ed. *Vatican Council II: The Conciliar and Postconciliar Documents*. Collegeville: Liturgical Press, 1975 and reprints. A convenient collection of the council documents, along with post-conciliar documents of direct relevance.

————. *Vatican Council II: The Basic Sixteen Documents. A New and Inclusive Language Translation of the Council Documents.* Northport, NY: Costello, 1996. A new translation in contemporary English.

————. *More Postconciliar Documents.* Northport, NY: Costello, 1998. A collection of additional important church documents issued after Vatican II.

Haught, John F. "Revelation." In *The New Dictionary of Theology*, ed. Joseph A. Komonchak, Mary Collins, and Dermot A. Lane, 884–99. Wilmington, DE: Michael Glazier, 1987. A broad overview of primary issues and major theological perspectives on the topic of revelation.

Lysik, David A., ed. *The Bible Documents: A Parish Resource.* Chicago: Liturgy Training Publications, 2001. A useful resource of the most important official Catholic documents on the Bible published in the twentieth century, including *Dei Verbum*; accompanied by explanatory introductions.

McBrien, Richard. *Catholicism, New Edition.* New York: HarperCollins, 1994. A large compendium of Catholic teaching, including a lengthy section on revelation (pp. 227–73).

Megivern, James J. *Bible Interpretation: Official Catholic Teachings.* Wilmington, NC: McGrath, 1978. An older but still useful collection of official Roman Catholic documents, in full text or excerpts, on biblical interpretation.

Miller, J. Michael, ed. *The Encyclicals of John Paul II.* Huntington, IN: Our Sunday Visitor, 1996. A collection of the pope's first thirteen encyclicals accompanied by useful introductions and brief analyses.

Navarro Lecanda, Angel María. *"Evangelii Traditio": Tradición como Evangelización a la Luz de Dei Verbum I–II*, 2 vols. Vitoria-Gasteiz: ESET, 1997. An extensive study of the first two chapters of *Dei Verbum*.

O'Collins, Gerald. "Revelation." In *The HarperCollins Encyclopedia of Catholicism*, Richard P. McBrien, gen. ed., 1112–14. New York: HarperCollins, 1995. A concise and informative analysis of principal teachings of *Dei Verbum*.

Tanner, Norman, ed. *Decrees of the Ecumenical Councils*, 2 vols. London: Sheed & Ward, subsequently Continuum / Washington, DC: Georgetown University Press, 1990. A superb collection of conciliar documents, from Nicaea I to Vatican II, with Latin/Greek and English texts on facing pages. For *Dei Verbum*, see vol. 2, 971–81.

Vorgrimler, Herbert, gen. ed. *Commentary on the Documents of Vatican II*, 5 vols. New York: Herder and Herder, 1967–1969. Still the best and most authoritative commentary on the origins and content of the various documents of the council. On *Dei Verbum*, see the essays of Joseph Ratzinger, Alois Grillmeier, and Béda Rigaux in vol. 3, 155–272.

GENERAL BIBLIOGRAPHY ON THE BIBLE,
REVELATION, AND CATHOLIC TEACHING

Baum, Gregory. "Vatican II's Constitution on Revelation: History and Interpretation." *TS* 28:1 (1967): 51–75. An excellent overview of the content of *Dei Verbum*.

Bertoldi, Francesco. "Henri de Lubac on Dei Verbum." *Communio: International Catholic Review* 17 (Spring 1990): 88–94. A good summary of de Lubac's positive assessment of *Dei Verbum* as promoting the unity of both the revealer and the revealed, Jesus Christ.

Bianchi, Enzo. "The Centrality of the Word of God." In *The Reception of Vatican II*, ed. Giuseppe Alberigo, Jean Pierre Jossua, and Joseph A. Komonchak, 115–36. Washington, DC: Catholic University Press, 1987. A brief rehearsal of the background and importance of *Dei Verbum*.

Brown, Raymond E. *Biblical Reflections on Crises Facing the Church*. New York: Paulist Press, 1975. A popular application of biblical interpretation to modern issues facing the church, including Christology, Mariology, catechetics, and ecumenism.

———. *The Critical Meaning of the Bible*. New York: Paulist Press, 1981. An insightful application of how the Bible can impact the life of the church.

———. *Biblical Exegesis and Church Doctrine*. New York/Mahwah, NJ: Paulist Press, 1985. Reprint, Eugene, OR.: Wipf and Stock, 2001. A clear and concise explanation of the interrelationship between biblical interpretation and church teaching.

Brown, Raymond E. and Thomas Aquinas Collins. "Church Pronouncements." In *The New Jerome Biblical Commentary*, ed. Raymond E. Brown, Joseph A. Fitzmyer, and Roland E. Murphy, §72:1166–74. Englewood Cliffs, NJ: Prentice-Hall, 1990. A convenient digest of Catholic teaching on the Bible in official documents throughout the church's history.

Collins, John J. and John Dominic Crossan, eds. *The Biblical Heritage in Modern Catholic Scholarship*. Wilmington, DE: Michael Glazier, 1986.

A collection of essays on the major parts of the Bible, in honor of Bruce Vawter, CM, a pioneer Catholic scholar in the mid-twentieth century.

Collins, Raymond F. "Rome and the Critical Study of the New Testament." In his *Introduction to the New Testament*, 356–86. Garden City, NY: Doubleday, 1983. An excellent, detailed history of Catholic interpretation of the Bible, especially the battles fought prior to and during Vatican II that had an impact on contemporary approaches to the Bible.

Donahue, John R. "Scripture: A Roman Catholic Perspective." *Review and Expositor* 79:2 (1982): 231–44. An excellent exposition of the importance of *Dei Verbum* nearly twenty years after its promulgation.

———. "Between Jerusalem and Athens: The Changing Shape of Catholic Biblical Scholarship." In *Hermes and Athena: Biblical Exegesis and Philosophical Theology*, ed. Eleonore Stump and Thomas P. Flint, 285–313. Notre Dame, IN: University of Notre Dame, 1993. The author's most thorough presentation of the state of Catholic biblical scholarship in the late twentieth century, with a proposal for the future.

———. "The Bible in Roman Catholicism since *Divino Afflante Spiritu*." *Word & World* 13:4 (1993): 404–13. A brief and perceptive historical overview of the development of a Catholic approach to the Bible.

———. "Catholic Biblical Scholarship Fifty Years after *Divino Afflante Spiritu*." *America* 169:7 (Sept. 18, 1993): 6–11. A popular summary of the author's views on the development of the Catholic approach to the Bible.

Dulles, Avery. *Models of Revelation*. Garden City, NY: Doubleday, 1983. A classic presentation of the complex theme of divine revelation, done by one of the outstanding American theologians of the twentieth century.

Fisichella, Rino. "*Dei Verbum Audiens et Proclamans*: On Scripture and Tradition as Source of the Word of God," *Communio* 28 (2001): 85–98. A good analysis of *Dei Verbum's* teaching about the relationship of Scripture and Tradition, with special emphasis on *Dei Verbum*, article 7.

✓ Fitzmyer, Joseph A. *Scripture, the Soul of Theology*. New York/Mahwah, NJ: Paulist Press, 1994. A fine set of essays on the interrelationship of Scripture and theology according to Vatican II.

———. *The Biblical Commission's Document "The Interpretation of the Bible in the Church": Text and Commentary*. SubBi 18; Rome: Pontifical Biblical

Institute, 1995. An authoritative explanation of this PBC document written by a premier American biblical scholar who himself was a member of the PBC.

———. "The Second Vatican Council and the Role of the Bible in Catholic Life." In *Faith, Word and Culture*, ed. Liam Bergin, 32–50. Co. Dublin: Columba Press, 2004. An incisive analysis of Vatican II's contribution to a Catholic approach to the Bible.

Fogarty, Gerald P. *American Catholic Biblical Scholarship: A History from the Early Republic to Vatican II*. San Francisco: Harper & Row, 1989. A superb historical study that includes an extensive analysis of *Dei Verbum* from an American perspective.

Frein, Brigid Curtin. "Scripture in the Life of the Church." In *Vatican II: The Continuing Agenda*, ed. Anthony J. Cernera, 71–87. Fairfield, CT: Sacred Heart University, 1997. A pithy summary of the impact of *Dei Verbum* on the Catholic Church.

Gaillardetz, Richard R. *By What Authority? A Primer on Scripture, the Magisterium, and the Sense of the Faithful*. Collegeville: Liturgical Press, 2003. The best popular explanation of the diverse levels of authoritative teaching in the Roman Catholic Church; includes chapters on revelation, inspiration, and biblical interpretation.

Harrington, Daniel J. "New Testament Study and Ministry of the Word." *ChicSt* 31 (1992): 117–29. A succinct statement of six challenges facing Catholic biblical interpretation in the wake of Vatican II.

———. "Catholic Interpretation of Scripture." In *The Bible in the Churches: How Different Christians Interpret the Scriptures*, 3d ed., ed. Kenneth Hagen, 29–59. New York/Mahwah, NJ: Paulist Press, 1998. An informative explanation of Catholic approaches to Scripture and current issues confronting the church on biblical interpretation.

———. *How Do Catholics Read the Bible?* Come and See Series. Lanham, MD: Rowman & Littlefield, 2005. A superb introduction to a Catholic approach to the Bible intended for non-specialists; each chapter begins with a quotation from *Dei Verbum* and ends with discussion/reflection questions.

Hegy, Pierre M., ed. *The Church in the Nineties: Its Legacy, Its Future*. Collegeville: Liturgical Press, 1993. Essays by various theologians from a conference held in 1990 in Washington, DC, to discuss Vatican II on the occasion of its twenty-fifth anniversary.

John Paul II. "Message on the Occasion of the 25th Anniversary of Dei Verbum." *Bulletin* Dei Verbum 18 (1991): 8, 13. The pope's encouraging message about the importance of the constitution in promoting awareness of the Bible.

Johnson, Luke Timothy and William S. Kurz. *The Future of Catholic Biblical Scholarship: A Constructive Conversation.* Grand Rapids: Eerdmans, 2002. A provocative proposal for a reconsideration of how Catholics should do biblical interpretation.

Lodge, John G. "*Dei Verbum* on Scripture and Tradition Forty Years Later," *ChicSt* 44:3 (2005): 238–49. A historical and theological review of the relationship between Scripture and Tradition according to *Dei Verbum.*

Mahoney, Edward J., ed. *Scripture as the Soul of Theology.* Collegeville: Liturgical Press, 2005. A small collection of essays by well-known Catholic scholars on modern Catholic theology, taking their inspiration from the teaching of Vatican II.

McGovern, Thomas J. "Magisterium, Scripture and Catholic exegetes, Part I." *HomPastRev* 91:10 (1991): 11–19; and "Magisterium, Scripture and Catholic exegetes, Part II." *HomPastRev* 91:11 (1991): 24–32, 71. A well-argued, conservative point of view about the proper interpretation of Vatican II on scriptural interpretation.

———. "Vatican II and the Interpretation of Scripture." *HomPastRev* 104:9 (2004): 6–16. A conservative yet balanced approach to the question of the impact of Vatican II on scriptural interpretation in the Catholic Church.

Miller, John H., ed. *Vatican II: An Interfaith Appraisal.* Notre Dame, IN: University of Notre Dame, 1966. An extensive record of an international theological conference held at the University of Notre Dame in March 1966 to assess the impact of Vatican II; on *Dei Verbum,* see especially pp. 43–88.

Moeser, Marion. "Overview of *Dei Verbum.*" In *The Bible Documents: A Parish Resource,* ed. David A. Lysik, 50–57. Chicago: Liturgy Training Publications, 2001. A good summary of the constitution, its strengths and its weaknesses.

Murphy, Roland E. "What Is Catholic about Catholic Biblical Scholarship?—Revisited." *BTB* 28:3 (1998): 112–19. Not so much a response to the Johnson-Kurz book above but an engagement of the same kinds of issues from a well-known and experienced Catholic exegete.

Neyrey, Jerome H. "Interpretation of Scripture in the Life of the Church." In *Vatican II: The Unfinished Agenda*, ed. Lucien Richard, Daniel J. Harrington, and John W. O'Malley, 33–46. Wilmington, DE: Michael Glazier, 1987. An insightful look at the strengths and weaknesses of *Dei Verbum* with a view toward outlining the unfinished agenda for a Catholic approach to the Bible.

Oakes, Edward T. "Was Vatican II a Liberal or Conservative Council?" *ChicSt* 43:2 (2004): 191–211. A re-evaluation of Vatican II from the viewpoint of the diverse theological positions represented at the council.

O'Collins, Gerald. "'Dei Verbum' and Biblical Scholarship." *Scripture Bulletin* 21 (1991) 2–7. A short overview of the impact of the constitution on biblical scholarship.

———. *Retrieving Fundamental Theology: The Three Styles of Contemporary Theology*. New York/Mahwah, NJ: Paulist Press, 1993. A well-done presentation of theological issues and *Dei Verbum*, including a chapter on the theme of revelation in the other documents from Vatican II and an indispensable appendix with an extensive bibliography on *Dei Verbum* (co-authored with Joseph Cassar, pp. 178–217).

Onaiyekan, John. "The Constitution *Dei Verbum* after 25 Years: CBF Perspective." *Bulletin* Dei Verbum 17/4 (1990): 4–11. A brief report on the importance of *Dei Verbum* in the context of the mission of Catholic Biblical Federation to promote dissemination of the Bible.

Osiek, Carolyn. "Catholic or catholic? Biblical Scholarship at the Center," *JBL* 125:1 (2006): 5–22. The author's presidential address to the Society of Biblical Literature given in November 2005, providing an insightful analysis of current issues in Catholic biblical scholarship.

✓ Ratzinger, Joseph. *Theological Highlights of Vatican II*. New York/Mahwah, NJ: Paulist Press, 1966. Discusses the early phases of *Dei Verbum* (pp. 20–26),

Sauer, Hanjo. "The Doctrinal and the Pastoral: The Text on Divine Revelation." In *History of Vatican II*, ed. Giuseppe Alberigo and Joseph A. Komonchak, vol. 4, 195–231. Maryknoll, NY: Orbis, 2003. Part of the definitive history of the council, this analysis summarizes many of the interventions concerning *Dei Verbum* as it went through successive drafts.

Senior, Donald. "Dogmatic Constitution on Divine Revelation." In *Vatican II and Its Documents: An Appraisal*, ed. Timothy E. O'Connell, 122–40. Theology and Life Series 15. Wilmington, DE: Michael Glazier, 1986. A concise and balanced assessment of *Dei Verbum* by one of the foremost contemporary American Catholic biblical scholars and now a member of the PBC.

Senior, Donald and Carroll Stuhlmueller. "American Catholicism and the Biblical Movement." In *Where We Are: American Catholics in the 1980's*, ed. Michael Glazier, 64–88. Wilmington, DE: Glazier, 1985. An early assessment of the issues confronting Catholic exegetes twenty years after the council.

Serratelli, Arthur. "Reflections on Revelation: *Dei Verbum's* 40th Anniversary." *Origins* 35:8 (July 7, 2005): 118–21. A short essay delivered at a conference at the University of Notre Dame by an American bishop and biblical scholar on the significance of *Dei Verbum*.

Stacpoole, Alberic, ed. *Vatican II Revisited by Those Who Were There*. Minneapolis: Winston Press, 1986. An interesting and informative collection of essays by participants on many aspects of the council.

Stuhlmueller, Carroll. "Vatican II and Biblical Criticism." In *The Impact of Vatican II*, ed. John Ford, et al., 27–43. St. Louis: B. Herder, 1966. A sympathetic yet critical early assessment of *Dei Verbum* shortly after the conclusion of the council.

Wicks, Jared. "Dei Verbum Developing." In *The Convergence of Theology: Festschrift for Gerald O'Collins*, ed. Daniel Kendall and Stephen T. Davis, 109–25. New York/Mahwah, NJ: Paulist Press, 2001. A detailed summary of the various phases in the production of the final text of *Dei Verbum*.

Williamson, Peter S. *Catholic Principles for Interpreting Scripture: A Study of the Pontifical Biblical Commission's* The Interpretation of the Bible in the Church. *SubBi* 22; Rome: Pontifical Biblical Institute, 2001. A dissertation that surveys methods used by Catholic scholars for Bible study, proposing twenty principles for Catholic exegesis and discussing an agenda for the future of Catholic biblical studies.

———. "Catholic Principles for Interpreting Scripture." *CBQ* 65 (2003): 327–49. A digest of the author's major points from his dissertation (see above).

Witherup, Ronald D. "Is There a Catholic Approach to Scripture?" *The Priest* 51:2 (1995): 29–35. An attempt to lay out the essentials of a Catholic approach to Scripture based upon *Dei Verbum* and beyond.

———. "Overview of *The Interpretation of the Bible in the Church*." In *The Bible Documents: A Parish Resource*, ed., David A. Lysik, 120–26. Chicago:

Liturgy Training Publications, 2001. A brief, popular introduction to the PBC document that contains the most extensive treatment of issues on biblical interpretation since Vatican II.

————. "The Incarnate Word Revealed: The Pastoral Writings of Raymond E. Brown." In *Life in Abundance: Studies of John's Gospel in Tribute to Raymond E. Brown*, ed. John R. Donahue, 238–52. Collegeville: Liturgical Press, 2005. A review of the impact of the pastoral writings since Vatican II of one of the foremost Catholic biblical scholars of the twentieth century.

————. "The Interpretation of the Bible in the Roman Catholic Church and the Orthodox Churches." In *Scripture: An Ecumenical Introduction to the Bible and Its Interpretation*, ed. Michael J. Gorman, 195–215. Peabody, MA: Hendrickson, 2005. A short summary of the major themes and issues in Catholic and Orthodox approaches to the Bible in the context of ecumenical discussions.

SCRIPTURE CITATIONS

INDEX